How To Retire And Be Happy

30 secrets to a happy, healthy, and wealthy retirement

By Eli'ezer Press

Copyright © 2024

By Eli'ezer Press

All rights reserved. No part of this publication may be reproduced, distributed, or transmitted in any form or by any means, including photocopying, recording, or other electronic or mechanical methods, without the prior written permission of the publisher, except in the case of brief quotations embodied in critical reviews and certain other noncommercial uses permitted by copyright law.

Table of Content

Copyright © 2024.. 2
Table of Content..4
Introduction... 10
Welcome to Your New Journey.. 10
   Overview of Retirement... 10
   Importance of Happiness, Health, and Wealth in Retirement.. 11
Part 1.. 14
Planning Your Retirement.. 14
Chapter 1.. 16
Secret 1: Start Planning Early... 16
   The Benefits of Early Retirement Planning.................. 16
   Setting Realistic Goals... 17
Chapter 2..20
Secret 2: Financial Planning and Budgeting..................... 20
   Creating a Retirement Budget.. 20
   Understanding Retirement Accounts and Investments....22
Chapter 3..26
Secret 3: Assessing Your Retirement Needs......................26
   Calculating Retirement Expenses.................................. 26
   Estimating Healthcare Costs...28
Chapter 4..32
Secret 4: Diversifying Your Income Streams.................... 32
   Exploring Passive Income Options................................32
   Rental Properties, Dividends, and Side Businesses.........34
Chapter 5..38

Secret 5: Managing Debt Before Retirement 38
    Strategies to Pay Off Debt 38
    Importance of Being Debt-Free 40
Part 2 Optimizing Your Retirement Income 44
Chapter 6 46
Secret 6: Maximizing Social Security Benefits 46
    When to Start Taking Benefits 46
    Strategies to Increase Benefits 48
Chapter 7 52
Secret 7: Smart Investing in Retirement 52
    Safe Investment Options 52
    Balancing Risk and Returns 54
Chapter 8 58
Secret 8: Creating a Sustainable Withdrawal Plan 58
    Safe Withdrawal Rates 58
    Ensuring Your Savings Last 60
Chapter 9 64
Secret 9: Understanding Taxes in Retirement 64
    Tax-Efficient Withdrawal Strategies 64
    Reducing Tax Liability 67
Chapter 10 70
Secret 10: Estate Planning 70
    Importance of Wills and Trusts 70
    Planning for Inheritance and Legacy 73
Part 3 Maintaining Physical Health 76
Chapter 11 78
Secret 11: Staying Physically Active 78
    Importance of Exercise 78

Developing a Fitness Routine..79
Chapter 12..84
Secret 12: Healthy Eating Habits.....................................84
    Nutritional Needs in Retirement....................................84
    Planning Balanced Meals..86
    Additional Tips..88
Chapter 13..90
Secret 13: Regular Health Check-ups and Screenings.....90
    Importance of Regular Health Check-ups.....................90
    Essential Health Screenings in Retirement...................91
    Tips for Making the Most of Your Health Check-ups.....94
Chapter 14..96
Secret 14: Mental Health and Wellness........................96
    Managing Stress and Anxiety..96
    Practicing Mindfulness and Meditation.......................97
Chapter 15..102
Secret 15: Adopting a Healthy Sleep Routine...............102
    Importance of Sleep..102
    Tips for Better Sleep...103
Part 4..108
Staying Engaged and Happy..108
Chapter 16..110
Secret 16: Finding a Purpose..110
    Discovering New Passions..110
    Volunteering and Community Service.........................111
    Additional Tips for Finding Purpose.............................113
Chapter 17..116
Secret 17: Building and Maintaining Relationships........116

Staying Connected with Family and Friends.................116
Meeting New People..118
Additional Tips for Building and Maintaining
Relationships.. 120

Chapter 18..122
Secret 18: Traveling and Exploring New Places...............122
Benefits of Travel in Retirement................................... 122
Planning Budget-Friendly Trips..................................... 124
Additional Tips for Enjoying Travel in Retirement........127

Chapter 19..130
Secret 19: Lifelong Learning..130
Taking Up New Hobbies and Interests........................... 130
Enrolling in Courses and Workshops............................. 132
Tips for Embracing Lifelong Learning........................... 133

Chapter 20..136
Secret 20: Giving Back to the Community........................136
Volunteering Opportunities..136
Impact of Community Service on Happiness.................138
Additional Tips for Volunteering....................................141

Part 5:...144
Personal Growth and Fulfillment............................ 144
Chapter 21..146
Secret 21: Practicing Gratitude.. 146
Importance of Gratitude...146
Keeping a Gratitude Journal.. 148
Additional Tips for Practicing Gratitude....................... 150

Chapter 22..152
Secret 22: Embracing Change and Adaptability.............152
Dealing with Life Changes.. 152

    Staying Flexible and Open-Minded................................ 154
Chapter 23..**158**
Secret 23: Simplifying Your Life..**158**
    Decluttering and Downsizing.. 158
    Focusing on What Truly Matters.................................... 161
Chapter 24..**166**
Secret 24: Pursuing Creative Outlets.................................**166**
    Engaging in Arts and Crafts... 166
    Exploring Music... 168
    Indulging in Writing... 170
Chapter 25..**174**
Secret 25: Strengthening Spirituality................................**174**
    Exploring Spiritual Practices.. 174
    Finding Inner Peace... 176
Part 6: Ensuring Long-Term Happiness..........................**180**
Chapter 26..**182**
Secret 26: Maintaining a Positive Attitude.......................**182**
    Power of Positive Thinking... 182
    Overcoming Negative Thoughts......................................184
Chapter 27..**188**
Secret 27: Setting New Goals and Challenges..................**188**
    Importance of Goal-Setting.. 188
    Taking on New Challenges... 190
Chapter 28..**194**
Secret 28: Celebrating Milestones and Achievements....**194**
    Acknowledging and Celebrating Successes................... 194
    Reflecting on Accomplishments.....................................196
Chapter 29..**200**

Secret 29: Creating a Legacy..200
    Making a Lasting Impact..200
    Documenting Your Life Story.. 202
Chapter 30..**206**
Secret 30: Enjoying the Journey......................................**206**
    Embracing the Joy of Retirement................................ 206
    Living in the Moment.. 208
Conclusion..**212**
    Looking Ahead.. 212
    Recap of Key Points... 214
    Encouragement and Final Thoughts............................. 215

Introduction

Welcome to Your New Journey

Retirement marks the beginning of an exciting new chapter in life, a time filled with opportunities to explore, relax, and enjoy the fruits of your labor. Whether you've eagerly anticipated this moment for years or you're just starting to contemplate what retirement might look like, this eBook is designed to guide you toward a fulfilling, joyful, and prosperous retirement.

Overview of Retirement

Retirement is often seen as a period of rest after decades of hard work, but it's much more than just an end to your professional career. It's a time to reinvent yourself, pursue passions, and create memories with loved ones. For many, retirement is an opportunity to explore hobbies, travel to new destinations, volunteer in the community, and even embark on new ventures.

However, the transition to retirement can also be challenging. Without the structure and social interactions of a regular job, some people find themselves feeling lost or unfulfilled. That's why it's essential to approach retirement with a well-rounded plan that addresses not only financial security but also your physical health and emotional well-being.

Importance of Happiness, Health, and Wealth in Retirement

To truly enjoy retirement, it's crucial to find a balance between happiness, health, and wealth. These three elements are interconnected and equally important for a satisfying retirement.

1. **Happiness**: Emotional well-being is at the core of a successful retirement. This means finding joy in everyday activities, maintaining strong relationships, and pursuing passions that give you a sense of purpose. Whether it's spending time with family, engaging in hobbies, or volunteering, staying mentally and emotionally engaged will significantly enhance your quality of life.
2. **Health**: Physical health is a key factor in enjoying a long and active retirement. Regular exercise, a balanced diet, and routine medical check-ups are essential to maintaining your health. By prioritizing your physical well-being, you can ensure that you're able to participate in the activities you love and minimize

health-related issues that could detract from your retirement experience.
3. **Wealth**: Financial security provides the foundation for a worry-free retirement. Proper financial planning, including budgeting, investing, and managing expenses, ensures that you have the resources to live comfortably and pursue your dreams. By taking control of your finances, you can reduce stress and focus on enjoying your retirement to the fullest.

This book will guide you through 30 secrets to achieving a happy, healthy, and wealthy retirement. Each chapter is packed with practical advice, actionable tips, and inspiring stories to help you navigate this exciting journey. Whether you're already retired or planning for the future, these insights will empower you to create the retirement of your dreams. Welcome to your new journey – let's make it an extraordinary one!

Part 1

Planning Your Retirement

Chapter 1

Secret 1: Start Planning Early

The Benefits of Early Retirement Planning

Starting your retirement planning early comes with a multitude of benefits that can significantly enhance your retirement experience. One of the most significant advantages is the power of compound interest. By beginning to save and invest early, your money has more time to grow. The earlier you start, the less you need to contribute regularly to reach your retirement goals, thanks to the compound interest working in your favor.

Another benefit of early planning is the ability to ride out market fluctuations. Financial markets can be unpredictable, with periods of volatility. However, by starting early, you have the luxury of time to weather these ups and downs. This long-term perspective reduces the stress associated with market volatility and provides a more stable financial foundation.

Early planning also allows for more flexibility in your retirement strategy. You have the time to explore different investment options, adjust your plans as needed, and take calculated risks that could lead to higher returns. This flexibility extends to your career choices as well. Knowing that you are on track for a comfortable retirement can give you the confidence to pursue job opportunities that you are passionate about, even if they come with lower salaries.

Moreover, starting early gives you ample time to address any financial gaps or challenges. Whether it's paying off debt, building an emergency fund, or saving for major expenses, having a long-term plan allows you to tackle these issues gradually, without overwhelming your current financial situation.

Setting Realistic Goals

Setting realistic retirement goals is a crucial component of early planning. These goals will guide your saving and investing strategies, ensuring that you are on the right track to achieve the retirement lifestyle you desire.

Begin by envisioning what your ideal retirement looks like. Consider factors such as where you want to live, the activities you want to engage in, and the lifestyle you wish to maintain. Do you plan to travel extensively, take up new hobbies, or spend more time with family and friends? Understanding your vision for retirement will help you determine the financial resources needed to support it.

Once you have a clear picture of your desired retirement, calculate the estimated costs associated with it. This includes everyday living expenses, healthcare costs, travel plans, and any other anticipated expenditures. Be realistic in your estimates and factor in inflation to ensure your calculations remain accurate over time.

With these estimates in hand, you can set specific, measurable, achievable, relevant, and time-bound (SMART) goals. For example, if you want to retire at age 65 with a certain amount of savings, break down this goal into smaller, manageable milestones. Determine how much you need to save annually or monthly to reach your target. This approach makes your goals more attainable and helps you stay motivated as you track your progress.

In addition to financial goals, consider setting personal goals that contribute to your overall well-being in retirement. This might include maintaining a healthy lifestyle, staying socially active, or pursuing lifelong learning opportunities. Balancing financial and personal goals ensures a holistic approach to retirement planning.

Starting your retirement planning early and setting realistic goals are fundamental steps toward a happy, healthy, and wealthy retirement. By taking these steps now, you can enjoy the peace of mind that comes with knowing you are prepared for the future, allowing you to fully embrace and enjoy the journey ahead.

Chapter 2

Secret 2: Financial Planning and Budgeting

Financial planning and budgeting are essential components of a successful retirement strategy. By carefully managing your finances, you can ensure that your resources last throughout your retirement years, allowing you to enjoy a worry-free and fulfilling retirement.

Creating a Retirement Budget

Creating a retirement budget is the first step in managing your finances effectively. A well-thought-out budget helps you understand your financial needs, control your spending, and make informed decisions about your retirement lifestyle.

1. **Calculate Your Income**: Begin by identifying all potential sources of income during retirement. This includes Social Security benefits, pensions, annuities, rental income, part-time work, and any other income streams. Having a clear picture of your income will help you determine how much

money you have available to cover your expenses.
2. **Estimate Your Expenses**: Next, estimate your monthly and annual expenses. Consider both fixed expenses (such as housing, utilities, insurance, and healthcare) and variable expenses (such as travel, entertainment, dining out, and hobbies). Be realistic in your estimates and account for inflation to ensure your budget remains accurate over time.
3. **Identify Discretionary Spending**: Separate your essential expenses from discretionary spending. Essential expenses are those that are necessary for daily living, while discretionary spending includes non-essential items and activities. This distinction will help you prioritize your spending and make adjustments if necessary.
4. **Plan for Healthcare Costs**: Healthcare is a significant expense in retirement. Make sure to include costs for Medicare premiums, supplemental insurance, prescription medications, and any out-of-pocket expenses. Planning for healthcare costs will help you avoid unexpected financial burdens.
5. **Account for Emergencies**: Set aside a portion of your budget for emergencies. Having an emergency fund ensures that you are prepared for unexpected expenses, such as home repairs or

medical emergencies, without disrupting your overall financial plan.
6. **Review and Adjust Regularly**: Your retirement budget is not a static document. Review it regularly and make adjustments as needed to reflect changes in your income, expenses, and financial goals. Staying flexible and proactive will help you stay on track and achieve your retirement objectives.

Understanding Retirement Accounts and Investments

Understanding the various retirement accounts and investment options available to you is crucial for effective financial planning. By making informed decisions about where to save and invest your money, you can maximize your returns and secure your financial future.

1. **Retirement Accounts**:
    - **401(k) and 403(b) Plans**: These employer-sponsored retirement plans allow you to contribute a portion of your pre-tax income, reducing your taxable income and growing your savings tax-deferred. Many employers also offer matching contributions, providing an

additional boost to your retirement savings.
- **Individual Retirement Accounts (IRAs)**: IRAs are personal retirement accounts that offer tax advantages. Traditional IRAs allow you to contribute pre-tax income and defer taxes until withdrawal, while Roth IRAs use after-tax income and offer tax-free withdrawals in retirement.
- **Pension Plans**: Some employers offer defined benefit pension plans that provide a guaranteed income in retirement based on your years of service and salary. Understanding your pension benefits and how they fit into your overall retirement plan is essential.

2. **Investment Options**:
    - **Stocks and Bonds**: Investing in stocks and bonds can provide growth and income for your retirement portfolio. Stocks offer potential for higher returns but come with higher risk, while bonds provide more stable, lower-risk income.
    - **Mutual Funds and ETFs**: Mutual funds and exchange-traded funds (ETFs) allow

you to diversify your investments across a range of assets, reducing risk and simplifying portfolio management.
- **Real Estate**: Real estate investments, such as rental properties or real estate investment trusts (REITs), can provide additional income and diversification for your retirement portfolio.
- **Annuities**: Annuities are insurance products that provide a guaranteed income stream in retirement. They can be a valuable tool for ensuring financial security, but it's important to understand the terms and fees associated with them.

3. **Risk Management and Diversification**: Balancing risk and reward is key to successful investing. Diversify your investments across different asset classes and sectors to reduce risk and protect your portfolio from market volatility. Regularly review your investment strategy and adjust it based on your risk tolerance and retirement goals.

4. **Professional Guidance**: Consider working with a financial advisor to develop a personalized retirement plan. A professional can help you navigate the complexities of retirement accounts, investments, and tax strategies, ensuring that your financial plan aligns with your long-term goals.

Effective financial planning and budgeting are the cornerstones of a secure and enjoyable retirement. By creating a comprehensive retirement budget and understanding your retirement accounts and investments, you can confidently manage your finances and focus on living a happy, healthy, and wealthy retirement.

Chapter 3

Secret 3: Assessing Your Retirement Needs

Assessing your retirement needs is a crucial step in ensuring that you have enough resources to enjoy a comfortable and fulfilling retirement. By calculating your retirement expenses and estimating healthcare costs, you can create a realistic financial plan that addresses all aspects of your future lifestyle.

Calculating Retirement Expenses

Calculating your retirement expenses involves taking a detailed look at your anticipated spending patterns to ensure that your savings and income will cover your needs. Here are the key steps to consider:

1. **Identify Your Current Expenses**: Start by reviewing your current spending habits. Categorize your expenses into fixed (necessary) and variable (discretionary) costs. Fixed expenses include housing, utilities, groceries, insurance, and transportation, while variable expenses encompass entertainment, dining out, travel, and hobbies.

2. **Project Future Spending**: Consider how your spending might change in retirement. Some expenses, like commuting or work-related costs, may decrease, while others, such as travel or leisure activities, might increase. Be realistic about how your lifestyle may evolve and adjust your projections accordingly.
3. **Adjust for Inflation**: Inflation can significantly impact your purchasing power over time. When estimating future expenses, account for an annual inflation rate. A common practice is to use a rate of 2-3% per year to ensure your calculations remain accurate.
4. **Consider Long-Term Goals and Projects**: Think about any significant goals or projects you might want to undertake in retirement, such as home renovations, major travel plans, or starting a new business. Include these one-time expenses in your overall calculations to ensure your budget can accommodate them.
5. **Include Emergency Funds**: Set aside a portion of your budget for unexpected expenses. Having an emergency fund helps you handle unforeseen financial challenges without derailing your retirement plan. Aim to save at least 3-6 months' worth of living expenses for emergencies.
6. **Regular Review and Adjustment**: Your retirement expenses may change over time, so it's

essential to review your budget regularly. Life events, market conditions, and changes in personal circumstances can all impact your financial needs. Adjust your budget as needed to stay on track.

Estimating Healthcare Costs

Healthcare is one of the most significant expenses in retirement, and accurately estimating these costs is vital for a comprehensive retirement plan. Here are the key factors to consider:

1. **Medicare Costs**: While Medicare provides essential health coverage for retirees, it doesn't cover all medical expenses. Understand the different parts of Medicare:
    - **Part A**: Hospital insurance, usually premium-free if you've paid Medicare taxes while working.
    - **Part B**: Medical insurance, which covers outpatient care, preventive services, and doctor visits. This requires a monthly premium.
    - **Part D**: Prescription drug coverage, which also involves a monthly premium.
2. **Supplemental Insurance**: Consider purchasing a Medicare Supplement (Medigap) policy to cover

out-of-pocket costs not covered by Medicare, such as copayments, coinsurance, and deductibles. Alternatively, you can opt for a Medicare Advantage Plan, which offers additional benefits.
3. **Out-of-Pocket Costs**: Estimate your out-of-pocket healthcare expenses, including premiums, deductibles, copayments, and coinsurance. Additionally, account for costs not covered by Medicare, such as dental, vision, hearing care, and long-term care.
4. **Long-Term Care**: Long-term care, such as nursing home care or in-home assistance, is a significant potential expense in retirement. Traditional health insurance and Medicare typically do not cover long-term care costs. Consider long-term care insurance to help manage these expenses or explore alternative strategies, such as hybrid life insurance policies with long-term care riders.
5. **Personal Health and Family History**: Your personal health and family medical history can influence your healthcare costs in retirement. Consider any chronic conditions or genetic predispositions when estimating future medical expenses. Maintaining a healthy lifestyle through regular exercise, a balanced diet, and preventive care can help mitigate some healthcare costs.

6. **Healthcare Savings Accounts (HSAs)**: If you're still working and have access to a Health Savings Account (HSA), take advantage of it. HSAs offer triple tax benefits: contributions are tax-deductible, earnings grow tax-free, and withdrawals for qualified medical expenses are tax-free. These accounts can be a valuable tool for covering healthcare costs in retirement.

By accurately assessing your retirement needs through careful calculation of expenses and thorough estimation of healthcare costs, you can create a robust financial plan that ensures your comfort and security. Being proactive in understanding and planning for these costs will empower you to enjoy a worry-free retirement.

Chapter 4

Secret 4: Diversifying Your Income Streams

Diversifying your income streams is a vital strategy for ensuring financial stability and resilience in retirement. Relying on a single source of income can be risky, as economic fluctuations or unforeseen circumstances may impact your financial security. By creating multiple streams of income, you can better manage risk and enjoy a more comfortable retirement.

Exploring Passive Income Options

Passive income is money earned with little to no ongoing effort. It can provide a steady cash flow, supplementing your primary retirement savings and helping to cover expenses. Here are several passive income options to consider:

1. **Dividend-Paying Stocks**: Investing in dividend-paying stocks allows you to earn regular income through dividends. Choose well-established companies with a history of paying consistent dividends. Reinvesting

dividends can further grow your investment portfolio.
2. **Real Estate Investments**: Rental properties can generate a reliable income stream. Whether you invest in residential or commercial real estate, rental income can provide steady cash flow. Consider hiring a property management company to handle day-to-day operations, making this a more passive investment.
3. **Real Estate Investment Trusts (REITs)**: If managing rental properties isn't for you, REITs offer an alternative way to invest in real estate. REITs are companies that own, operate, or finance income-generating real estate. They pay dividends to shareholders, providing a passive income stream.
4. **Bonds and Bond Funds**: Bonds are debt securities issued by corporations or governments. When you purchase a bond, you are lending money in exchange for periodic interest payments and the return of the principal amount at maturity. Bond funds pool money from many investors to buy a diversified portfolio of bonds, offering more stability and regular income.
5. **Peer-to-Peer Lending**: Peer-to-peer lending platforms connect borrowers with individual lenders. By lending money to borrowers, you can earn interest income. This option carries more

risk than traditional investments, so it's essential to research and diversify your lending portfolio.
6. **Royalties and Licensing**: If you have creative works, such as books, music, patents, or software, you can earn royalties or licensing fees. This income stream requires initial effort to create the work, but once established, it can provide ongoing revenue.

Rental Properties, Dividends, and Side Businesses

Beyond passive income options, consider diversifying your income streams through rental properties, dividends, and side businesses. These strategies can provide additional financial security and help you achieve your retirement goals.

1. **Rental Properties**: As mentioned earlier, rental properties can be a lucrative source of income. Consider the following tips for successful rental property investments:
    - **Location**: Choose properties in desirable locations with strong rental demand.
    - **Market Research**: Understand the local rental market, including average rent prices and vacancy rates.

- **Property Management**: Decide whether you will manage the property yourself or hire a property management company.
- **Maintenance and Upkeep**: Budget for ongoing maintenance and repairs to keep the property in good condition.

2. **Dividends**: Investing in dividend-paying stocks or funds can provide regular income. Consider the following strategies for dividend investing:
    - **Diversification**: Spread your investments across different sectors and industries to reduce risk.
    - **Reinvestment**: Reinvest dividends to compound your returns and grow your portfolio.
    - **Dividend Growth**: Look for companies with a history of increasing their dividends over time, providing potential for higher income.
3. **Side Businesses**: Starting a side business in retirement can be both financially rewarding and personally fulfilling. Consider the following ideas:
    - **Consulting or Freelancing**: Leverage your professional experience and skills to offer consulting or freelance services.

- **Online Businesses**: Explore opportunities in e-commerce, blogging, or creating online courses.
- **Hobbies and Crafts**: Turn your hobbies or crafts into a business by selling products or offering workshops.
- **Part-Time Work**: Consider part-time work that aligns with your interests and provides additional income.

By diversifying your income streams through passive income options, rental properties, dividends, and side businesses, you can create a more secure and resilient financial foundation for your retirement. These strategies not only provide financial benefits but also offer opportunities for personal growth and fulfillment.

Chapter 5

Secret 5: Managing Debt Before Retirement

Managing debt before retirement is crucial to ensuring a financially secure and stress-free retirement. Carrying significant debt into your retirement years can create financial strain and limit your ability to enjoy this new chapter of life. By implementing effective strategies to pay off debt and understanding the importance of being debt-free, you can set yourself up for a more comfortable and enjoyable retirement.

Strategies to Pay Off Debt

1. **Create a Debt Repayment Plan**: The first step in managing debt is to create a comprehensive repayment plan. List all your debts, including credit cards, mortgages, personal loans, and any other liabilities. For each debt, note the outstanding balance, interest rate, and minimum monthly payment. This will give you a clear picture of your total debt and help you prioritize which debts to tackle first.

2.   **Prioritize High-Interest Debt**: Focus on paying off high-interest debt first, such as credit card balances. These debts can quickly accumulate due to high interest rates, making them more costly over time. Use the avalanche method, where you make extra payments on the highest interest debt while continuing to pay the minimum on others. Once the highest interest debt is paid off, move on to the next highest.

3.   **Consider the Snowball Method**: Another popular debt repayment strategy is the snowball method. This approach involves paying off the smallest debts first, regardless of interest rate, to build momentum and motivation. As you eliminate smaller debts, you gain confidence and have more money to put towards larger debts.

4.   **Refinance or Consolidate Loans**: Refinancing or consolidating loans can lower your interest rates and simplify your debt repayment. By consolidating multiple high-interest debts into a single loan with a lower interest rate, you can reduce your monthly payments and pay off debt more efficiently. Be sure to shop around for the best terms and conditions.

5. **Increase Your Payments**: If possible, increase your monthly payments to accelerate debt repayment. Any extra money, such as bonuses, tax refunds, or windfalls, should be directed towards paying down debt. Even small additional payments can significantly reduce the overall interest paid and shorten the repayment period.

6. **Cut Unnecessary Expenses**: Review your budget and identify areas where you can cut unnecessary expenses. Redirect these savings towards debt repayment. By making sacrifices now, you can achieve a debt-free retirement sooner.

7. **Seek Professional Help**: If you are overwhelmed by debt or unsure how to proceed, consider seeking help from a financial advisor or credit counselor. These professionals can provide personalized advice and help you develop a realistic debt repayment plan.

Importance of Being Debt-Free

1. **Financial Freedom**: Being debt-free in retirement means you have more financial freedom and flexibility. Without the burden of monthly debt payments, you can allocate your

income towards enjoying your retirement, whether that means traveling, pursuing hobbies, or spending time with loved ones.

2. **Reduced Stress**: Debt can be a significant source of stress, particularly for retirees on a fixed income. Eliminating debt reduces financial stress and allows you to focus on your health, happiness, and overall well-being.

3. **Increased Savings**: Without debt payments, you can save more for future expenses and emergencies. Building a robust savings cushion ensures that you are prepared for unexpected costs, such as medical bills or home repairs, without resorting to taking on new debt.

4. **Enhanced Retirement Lifestyle**: A debt-free retirement allows you to maintain or even improve your standard of living. You can enjoy more discretionary spending and have the financial flexibility to take advantage of new opportunities and experiences.

5. **Legacy and Peace of Mind**: Eliminating debt provides peace of mind knowing that you won't leave financial burdens to your loved ones. This is particularly important if you have

dependents or wish to leave a financial legacy for your children or grandchildren.

6. **Better Health Outcomes**: Financial stress can negatively impact your physical and mental health. By managing debt and achieving financial stability, you can improve your overall health and well-being, leading to a happier and more fulfilling retirement.

Managing debt before retirement is a critical step in achieving financial security and peace of mind. By implementing effective debt repayment strategies and understanding the importance of being debt-free, you can create a solid financial foundation that allows you to fully enjoy the rewards of your retirement.

Part 2 Optimizing Your Retirement Income

Chapter 6

Secret 6: Maximizing Social Security Benefits

Maximizing your Social Security benefits is a crucial aspect of retirement planning. Understanding when to start taking benefits and implementing strategies to increase your benefits can significantly enhance your financial security and help you achieve a comfortable retirement.

When to Start Taking Benefits

1. **Know Your Full Retirement Age (FRA)**: Your Full Retirement Age (FRA) is the age at which you are entitled to receive your full Social Security benefit amount. FRA varies depending on your birth year. For those born between 1943 and 1954, the FRA is 66. For those born in 1960 or later, the FRA is 67. Understanding your FRA is essential for making informed decisions about when to start taking benefits.

2. **Early Retirement**: You can start taking Social Security benefits as early as age 62, but

your benefits will be permanently reduced by up to 30%, depending on your FRA. If you choose early retirement, you will receive a smaller monthly benefit for the rest of your life. However, starting benefits early may be beneficial if you need the income sooner or have a shorter life expectancy.

3. **Delayed Retirement**: Delaying Social Security benefits beyond your FRA can significantly increase your monthly benefit. For each year you delay benefits beyond your FRA, up to age 70, your benefit increases by approximately 8%. Delaying benefits can be advantageous if you have other sources of income and are in good health, as it maximizes your lifetime Social Security income.

4. **Consider Your Health and Longevity**: When deciding when to start taking benefits, consider your health and family history of longevity. If you are in good health and have a longer life expectancy, delaying benefits may result in higher lifetime income. Conversely, if you have health issues or a shorter life expectancy, starting benefits earlier may be more beneficial.

5. **Spousal Benefits**: If you are married, coordinating your Social Security claiming strategy with your spouse can maximize your combined benefits. Spouses are entitled to receive either their own benefit or up to 50% of their spouse's benefit, whichever is higher. Understanding how spousal benefits work can help you and your spouse make the best decision for your situation.

Strategies to Increase Benefits

1. **Work for at Least 35 Years**: Social Security benefits are calculated based on your highest 35 years of earnings. If you work fewer than 35 years, zeros will be averaged into your benefit calculation, reducing your monthly benefit. Working for at least 35 years ensures that you maximize your earnings history and, consequently, your benefits.

2. **Maximize Earnings**: Higher lifetime earnings result in higher Social Security benefits. Aim to maximize your earnings, especially during your highest-earning years. If possible, seek opportunities for raises, promotions, or additional income through part-time work or side businesses.

3.   **Avoid Early Retirement Penalties**: If you retire before your FRA and continue to work, your Social Security benefits may be temporarily reduced if your earnings exceed certain limits. In 2024, for example, the earnings limit is $21,240, and benefits are reduced by $1 for every $2 earned above this limit. After reaching your FRA, these penalties no longer apply, and your benefits are recalculated to credit you for any withheld amounts.

4.   **Take Advantage of Delayed Retirement Credits**: As mentioned earlier, delaying your benefits beyond your FRA can increase your monthly benefit by approximately 8% per year, up to age 70. This increase is known as delayed retirement credits. By waiting until age 70 to claim benefits, you can receive the maximum possible benefit.

5.   **Coordinate Benefits with Your Spouse**: Married couples have several strategies to maximize their combined Social Security benefits. For example, one spouse can claim spousal benefits while the other delays their own benefits to earn delayed retirement credits. This strategy allows couples to receive some income while maximizing their long-term benefits.

6. **Utilize Survivor Benefits**: If you are widowed, you may be eligible for survivor benefits, which are based on your deceased spouse's earnings record. Survivor benefits can start as early as age 60 (age 50 if disabled). If your own benefit is higher, you can switch to your own benefit at a later age. Understanding and planning for survivor benefits can help maximize your overall Social Security income.

7. **Understand Tax Implications**: Up to 85% of your Social Security benefits may be subject to federal income tax, depending on your combined income. Be aware of the tax implications of your Social Security benefits and consider strategies to minimize taxes, such as managing other sources of retirement income and utilizing tax-advantaged accounts.

Chapter 7

Secret 7: Smart Investing in Retirement

Smart investing in retirement is essential to ensure that your savings continue to grow and provide a steady income while protecting your capital. Understanding safe investment options and how to balance risk and returns can help you maintain financial security throughout your retirement years.

Safe Investment Options

1. **Bonds**: Bonds are debt securities issued by governments, municipalities, and corporations. They are generally considered safer investments compared to stocks because they offer fixed interest payments and return the principal at maturity. Government bonds, particularly U.S. Treasury bonds, are among the safest because they are backed by the government. Corporate bonds carry higher risk but offer higher yields. Diversifying your bond investments can help manage risk.

2.   **Certificates of Deposit (CDs)**: CDs are time deposits offered by banks and credit unions. They provide a fixed interest rate for a specified term, typically ranging from a few months to several years. CDs are low-risk investments insured by the Federal Deposit Insurance Corporation (FDIC) up to $250,000 per depositor, per institution. They are ideal for retirees seeking predictable, stable returns.

3.   **Annuities**: Annuities are insurance products that provide a guaranteed income stream for life or a specified period. They come in various forms, such as fixed annuities, which offer regular, fixed payments, and variable annuities, which provide payments that fluctuate based on the performance of underlying investments. Fixed annuities are considered safer, while variable annuities carry more risk but have the potential for higher returns.

4.   **Money Market Accounts**: Money market accounts are similar to savings accounts but typically offer higher interest rates and limited check-writing privileges. They are low-risk, liquid investments insured by the FDIC up to $250,000 per depositor, per institution. Money market funds, which invest in short-term,

high-quality securities, are another option, though they are not FDIC-insured.

5. **Dividend-Paying Stocks**: While stocks are generally riskier than bonds and CDs, dividend-paying stocks from well-established companies can provide a steady income stream with the potential for capital appreciation. Companies with a history of stable and growing dividends are often more resilient during market downturns. Diversifying your stock portfolio can help mitigate risk.

6. **Real Estate Investment Trusts (REITs)**: REITs invest in income-generating real estate properties and are required to distribute a significant portion of their income as dividends. They offer a way to invest in real estate without the complexities of property management. REITs can provide regular income and potential for capital appreciation, though they carry risks related to the real estate market.

Balancing Risk and Returns

1. **Diversification**: Diversification is the cornerstone of a balanced investment strategy. By spreading your investments across different asset classes (stocks, bonds, real estate, etc.) and

sectors, you reduce the risk of significant losses from any single investment. A well-diversified portfolio can provide more stable returns over time.

2. **Asset Allocation**: Determine an appropriate asset allocation based on your risk tolerance, financial goals, and time horizon. Generally, retirees should allocate a larger portion of their portfolio to lower-risk investments, such as bonds and fixed-income securities, while maintaining some exposure to growth-oriented assets, such as stocks, to hedge against inflation and ensure long-term growth.

3. **Regular Portfolio Reviews**: Conduct regular reviews of your investment portfolio to ensure it aligns with your risk tolerance and financial goals. Rebalance your portfolio as needed to maintain your desired asset allocation. This may involve selling some investments that have performed well and buying more of those that have underperformed.

4. **Inflation Protection**: Protect your portfolio from inflation by including investments that tend to perform well in inflationary environments. Treasury Inflation-Protected Securities (TIPS), real estate, and certain

commodities can help preserve your purchasing power over time.

5. **Risk Management**: Understand and manage the risks associated with your investments. This includes market risk, interest rate risk, inflation risk, and credit risk. Employ strategies such as dollar-cost averaging, which involves investing a fixed amount regularly regardless of market conditions, to mitigate the impact of market volatility.

6. **Professional Advice**: Consider working with a financial advisor to develop and implement a personalized investment strategy. A professional can provide valuable insights, help you navigate complex investment options, and ensure that your portfolio aligns with your long-term goals and risk tolerance.

Smart investing in retirement involves finding the right balance between protecting your capital and achieving adequate returns to sustain your lifestyle. By exploring safe investment options and implementing a diversified, well-managed investment strategy, you can enjoy financial security and peace of mind throughout your retirement years.

Chapter 8

Secret 8: Creating a Sustainable Withdrawal Plan

Creating a sustainable withdrawal plan is critical to ensuring that your retirement savings last throughout your retirement years. By understanding safe withdrawal rates and implementing strategies to manage your withdrawals, you can achieve financial stability and peace of mind.

Safe Withdrawal Rates

1. **The 4% Rule**: One of the most well-known guidelines for determining a safe withdrawal rate is the 4% rule. This rule suggests that you can withdraw 4% of your retirement savings in the first year of retirement and adjust that amount annually for inflation. This strategy is based on historical data indicating that a 4% withdrawal rate allows a portfolio to last for at least 30 years in most market conditions.

2. **Adjusting for Market Conditions**: While the 4% rule provides a general guideline, it's important to adjust your withdrawal rate

based on market performance and economic conditions. In years when your investments perform well, you might withdraw slightly more, while in years of poor performance, you might reduce your withdrawals to preserve your principal.

3. **Dynamic Withdrawal Strategies**: Consider adopting a dynamic withdrawal strategy that adjusts your annual withdrawals based on your portfolio's performance. For example, you might use a percentage-based approach, withdrawing a fixed percentage of your portfolio's value each year. This method helps ensure that you don't deplete your savings too quickly during market downturns.

4. **Bucket Strategy**: The bucket strategy involves dividing your retirement savings into different "buckets" based on when you'll need the money. Typically, you might have three buckets: one for short-term needs (1-3 years), one for medium-term needs (4-10 years), and one for long-term needs (10+ years). The short-term bucket contains low-risk, liquid investments, while the medium and long-term buckets contain a mix of growth-oriented and income-generating investments. This approach helps manage risk and provides a more predictable income stream.

5. **Consider Longevity**: With increasing life expectancies, it's essential to plan for a potentially long retirement. Being conservative with your withdrawal rate can help ensure that your savings last for 30 years or more. Consider factors such as your health, family history, and lifestyle when determining a sustainable withdrawal rate.

Ensuring Your Savings Last

1. **Create a Budget**: Develop a detailed retirement budget that outlines your expected expenses, including basic living costs, healthcare, travel, and leisure activities. Having a clear understanding of your expenses will help you determine a realistic withdrawal rate and ensure you live within your means.

2. **Minimize Withdrawals in Early Retirement**: If possible, try to minimize your withdrawals in the early years of retirement. This allows your investments more time to grow, increasing the likelihood that your savings will last. Consider part-time work or other income sources to reduce the need for large withdrawals initially.

3. **Monitor and Adjust**: Regularly review your financial situation and adjust your withdrawal plan as needed. Monitor your investment performance, expenses, and changes in your lifestyle to ensure your plan remains sustainable. Be prepared to make adjustments in response to market fluctuations, unexpected expenses, or changes in your financial goals.

4. **Emergency Fund**: Maintain an emergency fund to cover unexpected expenses without dipping into your retirement savings. An emergency fund helps you manage unforeseen costs, such as medical bills or home repairs, without compromising your long-term financial security.

5. **Tax-Efficient Withdrawals**: Plan your withdrawals to minimize taxes and maximize your after-tax income. For example, consider withdrawing from taxable accounts first, followed by tax-deferred accounts (like traditional IRAs and 401(k)s), and finally tax-free accounts (like Roth IRAs). This strategy can help reduce your overall tax burden and extend the life of your savings.

6. **Healthcare Costs**: Plan for healthcare costs, which can be a significant expense in

retirement. Consider long-term care insurance to cover potential long-term care needs. Factor in Medicare premiums, out-of-pocket costs, and other medical expenses when creating your withdrawal plan.

7. **Social Security and Pensions**: Coordinate your withdrawal plan with other sources of income, such as Social Security benefits and pensions. Delaying Social Security benefits can increase your monthly income and reduce the need to draw from your savings. Understand how your pension payments fit into your overall income strategy.

8. **Investment Strategy**: Maintain a diversified investment portfolio to balance risk and returns. A mix of stocks, bonds, and other assets can provide growth potential while generating income. Adjust your asset allocation based on your age, risk tolerance, and market conditions to ensure your portfolio supports your withdrawal plan.

Creating a sustainable withdrawal plan involves understanding safe withdrawal rates, carefully managing your expenses, and regularly reviewing your financial situation. By implementing these strategies, you can ensure that your retirement savings last, providing you with financial security and peace of mind throughout your retirement years.

Chapter 9

Secret 9: Understanding Taxes in Retirement

Understanding taxes in retirement is crucial for preserving your hard-earned savings and ensuring a steady income. By employing tax-efficient withdrawal strategies and reducing your tax liability, you can maximize your retirement income and maintain financial stability.

Tax-Efficient Withdrawal Strategies

1. **Know Your Tax Bracket**: Understanding your tax bracket is essential for planning tax-efficient withdrawals. Your taxable income determines your tax bracket, and by managing your withdrawals strategically, you can minimize the taxes owed. Be aware of the thresholds for different tax brackets to avoid pushing yourself into a higher bracket unnecessarily.

2. **Withdraw from Taxable Accounts First**: Generally, it's advisable to withdraw from taxable accounts, such as brokerage accounts, before tapping into tax-deferred accounts like

traditional IRAs and 401(k)s. This allows your tax-deferred accounts to continue growing tax-free for a longer period. Additionally, capital gains from taxable accounts may be taxed at lower rates compared to ordinary income from tax-deferred accounts.

3. **Utilize Roth Accounts**: Roth IRAs and Roth 401(k)s offer tax-free withdrawals in retirement, provided you meet the necessary requirements (e.g., the account has been open for at least five years, and you are over 59½). Including Roth accounts in your retirement savings strategy can provide significant tax benefits and offer more flexibility in managing your tax liability.

4. **Take Required Minimum Distributions (RMDs) Wisely**: At age 72, you must start taking RMDs from traditional IRAs and 401(k)s. Failure to take RMDs results in a hefty penalty—50% of the amount that should have been withdrawn. Plan your RMDs to minimize the impact on your tax bracket. If you have multiple tax-deferred accounts, consider consolidating them to simplify RMD calculations and management.

5. **Consider a Roth Conversion**: Converting a portion of your traditional IRA or

401(k) to a Roth IRA can be a tax-efficient strategy, especially if you anticipate being in a higher tax bracket in the future. You will pay taxes on the converted amount now, but future withdrawals from the Roth IRA will be tax-free. Timing and the amount of the conversion are critical to minimizing the tax impact.

6. **Tax-Loss Harvesting**: If you have investments in taxable accounts that have lost value, consider tax-loss harvesting. This involves selling the investments at a loss to offset gains from other investments, thereby reducing your taxable income. You can then reinvest the proceeds in similar assets to maintain your portfolio's balance.

7. **Utilize Standard and Itemized Deductions**: Make the most of standard deductions and itemized deductions to reduce your taxable income. Common deductions for retirees include medical expenses, charitable contributions, and mortgage interest. Plan your charitable giving and medical expenses to maximize your deductions in specific years.

Reducing Tax Liability

1. **Charitable Contributions**: Donating to qualified charities not only supports causes you care about but also provides tax benefits. If you are over 70½, consider making Qualified Charitable Distributions (QCDs) directly from your IRA to a charity. QCDs can satisfy your RMD requirements and are excluded from your taxable income.

2. **Health Savings Accounts (HSAs)**: If you have a high-deductible health plan, contribute to an HSA, which offers triple tax benefits: contributions are tax-deductible, earnings grow tax-free, and withdrawals for qualified medical expenses are tax-free. In retirement, HSAs can be used to pay for a wide range of healthcare expenses, reducing your overall tax burden.

3. **Timing Income and Deductions**: Manage the timing of your income and deductions to minimize taxes. For instance, if you anticipate a higher income year, defer certain income or accelerate deductible expenses to reduce your taxable income. Conversely, if you expect a lower income year, consider accelerating income or deferring deductions.

4.   **Social Security Benefits**: Be aware that a portion of your Social Security benefits may be taxable, depending on your combined income (adjusted gross income + nontaxable interest + half of your Social Security benefits). Plan your withdrawals from other accounts to manage your combined income and minimize the taxation of your Social Security benefits.

5.   **State Taxes**: Consider the state tax implications of your retirement income. Some states do not tax Social Security benefits or provide favorable tax treatment for retirement income. If you are flexible with your living arrangements, moving to a tax-friendly state can significantly reduce your overall tax liability.

6.   **Gifting**: Utilize the annual gift tax exclusion to transfer wealth to your heirs without incurring gift taxes. In 2024, you can gift up to $17,000 per person per year without triggering gift tax. Gifting can reduce the size of your taxable estate and provide financial support to your loved ones.

7.   **Professional Advice**: Work with a tax advisor or financial planner to develop and implement tax-efficient strategies tailored to your situation. Professional advice can help you

navigate complex tax laws, optimize your withdrawals, and reduce your overall tax liability.

Understanding taxes in retirement and implementing tax-efficient withdrawal strategies are essential for maximizing your retirement income and preserving your savings. By carefully managing your withdrawals and reducing your tax liability, you can achieve financial stability and enjoy a more comfortable and secure retirement.

Chapter 10

Secret 10: Estate Planning

Estate planning is a crucial aspect of retirement that ensures your assets are distributed according to your wishes and provides for your loved ones after your passing. Proper estate planning involves creating wills and trusts, as well as planning for inheritance and legacy. Understanding these elements can help you achieve peace of mind and ensure your family's financial security.

Importance of Wills and Trusts

1. **Wills**: A will is a legal document that outlines how you want your assets distributed after your death. It allows you to specify who will inherit your property, name guardians for minor children, and appoint an executor to manage your estate. Without a will, your assets will be distributed according to state laws, which may not align with your wishes. Key benefits of having a will include:
    - **Clarity**: A will provides clear instructions on how your assets should be distributed, reducing potential conflicts among heirs.

- **Control**: You have control over who receives your assets, ensuring they go to the people and causes you care about.
- **Guardianship**: If you have minor children, you can designate a guardian to care for them, providing for their well-being.
- **Executor**: You can appoint a trusted person to oversee the distribution of your estate and ensure your wishes are carried out.

2. **Trusts**: Trusts are legal arrangements where one party (the trustee) holds and manages assets on behalf of another party (the beneficiary). Trusts can be more flexible and private than wills and can provide additional benefits such as:
   - **Avoiding Probate**: Assets placed in a trust bypass the probate process, allowing for a faster and more private transfer to beneficiaries.
   - **Asset Protection**: Trusts can protect assets from creditors, lawsuits, and divorce settlements, ensuring they remain available for your beneficiaries.
   - **Tax Benefits**: Certain types of trusts can provide tax advantages, helping to preserve more of your estate for your heirs.

- **Control Over Distribution**: Trusts allow you to set specific terms for how and when your assets are distributed, which can be particularly useful for minor or financially inexperienced beneficiaries.
3. **Types of Trusts**:
    - **Revocable Living Trusts**: These trusts allow you to maintain control over your assets during your lifetime and make changes as needed. Upon your death, the assets are distributed according to the trust's terms, avoiding probate.
    - **Irrevocable Trusts**: Once established, these trusts cannot be altered. They offer greater asset protection and tax benefits but require you to give up control over the assets.
    - **Special Needs Trusts**: These trusts are designed to provide for a disabled beneficiary without affecting their eligibility for government benefits.
    - **Charitable Trusts**: These trusts allow you to leave a legacy by donating to charitable causes while potentially receiving tax benefits.

Planning for Inheritance and Legacy

1. **Identify Your Goals**: Consider what you want to achieve with your estate plan. This may include providing for your family's financial security, supporting charitable causes, or ensuring your business continues smoothly. Clearly defining your goals will help guide your estate planning decisions.
2. **Evaluate Your Assets**: Take an inventory of your assets, including real estate, investments, retirement accounts, life insurance policies, and personal property. Understanding the value and nature of your assets is essential for effective estate planning.
3. **Consider Tax Implications**: Estate taxes can significantly reduce the amount passed on to your heirs. Work with a financial advisor or estate planner to understand the tax implications of your estate and explore strategies to minimize taxes, such as gifting, charitable donations, and the use of trusts.
4. **Communicate with Your Family**: Discuss your estate plan with your family to ensure they understand your wishes and the reasons behind your decisions. Open communication can help prevent misunderstandings and conflicts after your passing.

5. **Update Beneficiary Designations**: Review and update the beneficiary designations on your retirement accounts, life insurance policies, and other financial accounts. These designations take precedence over your will, so it's crucial they align with your overall estate plan.
6. **Plan for Incapacity**: In addition to planning for your death, consider what will happen if you become incapacitated. Establish powers of attorney for financial and healthcare decisions to ensure your affairs are managed according to your wishes if you are unable to do so yourself.
7. **Leave a Legacy**: Think about how you want to be remembered and the impact you want to have on future generations. This might include charitable giving, creating scholarships, or establishing a family foundation. A well-thought-out legacy plan can reflect your values and make a lasting difference.
8. **Regularly Review and Update Your Plan**: Life changes such as marriage, divorce, the birth of children, or changes in financial status can affect your estate plan. Regularly review and update your plan to ensure it remains aligned with your goals and current circumstances.

Estate planning is a vital part of preparing for retirement. By creating a will and trusts, planning for inheritance, and leaving a legacy, you can ensure your assets are distributed according to your wishes, provide for your loved ones, and make a lasting impact. Proper estate planning provides peace of mind, knowing that you have taken steps to secure your family's future and preserve your legacy.

Part 3
Maintaining Physical Health

Chapter 11

Secret 11: Staying Physically Active

Maintaining physical health is crucial for enjoying a happy and fulfilling retirement. Staying physically active not only improves your overall well-being but also enhances your quality of life. This section explores the importance of exercise and provides tips for developing a fitness routine that suits your lifestyle and abilities.

Importance of Exercise

1. **Enhances Physical Health**: Regular exercise helps maintain a healthy weight, improves cardiovascular health, strengthens muscles and bones, and boosts flexibility and balance. This can reduce the risk of chronic diseases such as heart disease, diabetes, and osteoporosis, and can help manage conditions like arthritis and high blood pressure.
2. **Improves Mental Health**: Exercise has a significant positive impact on mental health. It reduces symptoms of anxiety and depression, improves mood, and enhances cognitive function. Physical activity releases endorphins, the body's

natural mood lifters, and promotes better sleep, which is essential for mental well-being.
3. **Increases Longevity**: Studies have shown that regular physical activity can increase life expectancy. By staying active, you can improve your chances of living a longer, healthier life, allowing you to enjoy more of your retirement years.
4. **Boosts Energy Levels**: Regular exercise can increase your energy levels by improving your cardiovascular system's efficiency. Enhanced blood flow and oxygen delivery to tissues help you feel more energetic and less fatigued.
5. **Social Benefits**: Participating in group exercise activities, sports, or fitness classes can provide social interaction, which is important for mental and emotional health. Building a social network through physical activity can reduce feelings of loneliness and isolation.

Developing a Fitness Routine

1. **Assess Your Fitness Level**: Before starting any exercise program, assess your current fitness level. Consider consulting with your doctor, especially if you have any chronic health conditions or concerns. Understanding your

starting point will help you set realistic goals and choose appropriate activities.
2. **Set Realistic Goals**: Establish clear, achievable fitness goals based on your assessment. Goals can include improving cardiovascular health, increasing strength, enhancing flexibility, or losing weight. Having specific, measurable goals can keep you motivated and focused.
3. **Choose Enjoyable Activities**: Select physical activities that you enjoy, as you're more likely to stick with them. Options include walking, swimming, cycling, yoga, dancing, gardening, or joining a local sports club. Mixing up your activities can keep your routine interesting and prevent boredom.
4. **Start Slowly and Progress Gradually**: If you're new to exercise or haven't been active for a while, start slowly to avoid injury and gradually increase the intensity and duration of your workouts. Begin with low-impact activities like walking or swimming and slowly incorporate more challenging exercises.
5. **Incorporate Different Types of Exercise**: A well-rounded fitness routine includes various types of exercise:
    - **Aerobic Exercise**: Activities like walking, jogging, cycling, or swimming improve cardiovascular health and

endurance. Aim for at least 150 minutes of moderate aerobic activity or 75 minutes of vigorous activity per week.
- **Strength Training**: Exercises like lifting weights, using resistance bands, or body-weight exercises (push-ups, squats) build and maintain muscle mass, which is important for overall strength and metabolism. Aim to include strength training exercises at least two days per week.
- **Flexibility and Balance Exercises**: Activities like yoga, Pilates, or tai chi improve flexibility, balance, and coordination, reducing the risk of falls and injuries. Incorporate these exercises into your routine several times a week.

6. **Create a Schedule**: Establish a regular exercise schedule that fits into your daily routine. Consistency is key to maintaining a fitness habit. Consider setting aside specific times each day for physical activity and treating them as non-negotiable appointments.
7. **Stay Hydrated and Eat Well**: Proper nutrition and hydration are essential for supporting your exercise routine. Drink plenty of water before, during, and after workouts. Eat a balanced diet

rich in fruits, vegetables, lean proteins, and whole grains to fuel your body and aid recovery.
8. **Listen to Your Body**: Pay attention to how your body responds to exercise. It's normal to feel some discomfort when starting a new routine, but persistent pain or discomfort should be addressed. Adjust your activities as needed and consult a healthcare professional if necessary.
9. **Track Your Progress**: Keep a record of your workouts, noting the types of exercises, duration, and intensity. Tracking your progress can help you stay motivated and identify areas for improvement. Celebrate your achievements and milestones along the way.
10. **Stay Motivated**: Maintaining motivation can be challenging, but finding ways to stay inspired is crucial. Join a fitness class or group, set new goals, reward yourself for reaching milestones, and remind yourself of the benefits of staying active.

Chapter 12

Secret 12: Healthy Eating Habits

Maintaining healthy eating habits is essential for overall well-being in retirement. Proper nutrition supports physical health, enhances cognitive function, and boosts energy levels. By understanding the nutritional needs in retirement and planning balanced meals, you can enjoy a vibrant and healthy lifestyle.

Nutritional Needs in Retirement

1. **Caloric Needs**: As you age, your metabolism slows down, and you may require fewer calories than in your younger years. However, it's crucial to ensure that the calories you consume are nutrient-dense, providing essential vitamins and minerals without excessive empty calories.

2. **Protein**: Adequate protein intake is vital for maintaining muscle mass, which naturally declines with age. Protein also supports immune function and helps repair tissues. Include a variety of protein sources in your diet, such as

lean meats, fish, eggs, dairy products, beans, and nuts.

3. **Calcium and Vitamin D**: These nutrients are essential for bone health, which becomes increasingly important as you age. Calcium-rich foods include dairy products, leafy greens, and fortified foods. Vitamin D can be obtained from sunlight, fatty fish, and fortified foods. Supplements may be necessary if dietary intake is insufficient.

4. **Fiber**: Fiber aids digestion, prevents constipation, and helps control blood sugar levels. Include plenty of fruits, vegetables, whole grains, and legumes in your diet to ensure adequate fiber intake.

5. **Healthy Fats**: Incorporate healthy fats, such as those found in avocados, nuts, seeds, and olive oil, to support heart health and reduce inflammation. Limit saturated and trans fats, which can increase the risk of heart disease.

6. **Hydration**: Staying hydrated is crucial for overall health. As you age, your sense of thirst may diminish, making it important to consciously drink enough water throughout the

day. Aim for at least 8 cups of water daily, more if you are physically active.

7. **Vitamins and Minerals**: A well-balanced diet should provide most of the vitamins and minerals you need. Pay particular attention to vitamins B12 and B6, which are essential for brain function and can be harder to absorb with age. Leafy greens, whole grains, and fortified cereals are good sources.

Planning Balanced Meals

1. **Meal Planning**: Planning your meals in advance ensures that you incorporate a variety of nutrient-dense foods into your diet. It also helps you avoid unhealthy choices and manage portion sizes.

2. **Balanced Breakfast**: Start your day with a balanced breakfast that includes protein, whole grains, and fruits or vegetables. Examples include oatmeal topped with nuts and berries, a vegetable omelet with whole-grain toast, or yogurt with fruit and granola.

3. **Nutritious Lunch**: For lunch, aim for a mix of lean protein, whole grains, and vegetables. Consider a quinoa salad with grilled chicken and

mixed vegetables, a turkey and avocado sandwich on whole-grain bread, or a lentil soup with a side of fresh fruit.

4. **Healthy Snacks**: Choose snacks that provide sustained energy and essential nutrients. Examples include a handful of nuts, sliced vegetables with hummus, a piece of fruit, or whole-grain crackers with cheese.

5. **Balanced Dinner**: Dinner should include a variety of food groups. Opt for grilled fish or chicken, a serving of whole grains like brown rice or quinoa, and a generous portion of steamed or roasted vegetables. Include a side salad for added fiber and nutrients.

6. **Portion Control**: Be mindful of portion sizes to avoid overeating. Use smaller plates and bowls to help manage portions and prevent excessive calorie intake. Focus on listening to your body's hunger and fullness cues.

7. **Cooking Methods**: Choose healthy cooking methods such as grilling, baking, steaming, or sautéing with minimal oil. Avoid deep-frying and excessive use of butter or high-calorie sauces.

8. **Variety and Color**: Incorporate a variety of colorful fruits and vegetables into your meals. Different colors indicate different nutrients, and eating a rainbow of produce ensures a wide range of vitamins and minerals.

9. **Limit Processed Foods**: Minimize the consumption of processed and packaged foods, which often contain high levels of sodium, sugar, and unhealthy fats. Opt for whole, unprocessed foods whenever possible.

10. **Enjoy Your Meals**: Take the time to enjoy your meals without distractions. Eating mindfully can improve digestion and help you better appreciate the flavors and textures of your food.

Additional Tips

1. **Read Labels**: Pay attention to nutrition labels on packaged foods to make informed choices. Look for products with lower sodium, sugar, and unhealthy fats.

2. **Stay Active**: Combine healthy eating with regular physical activity to maintain overall health and well-being.

3. **Consult Professionals**: If you have specific dietary needs or health conditions, consult a registered dietitian or nutritionist for personalized advice and meal planning.

4. **Social Eating**: Enjoy meals with family and friends to make eating a pleasurable and social experience. Sharing meals can also provide emotional support and strengthen relationships.

Healthy eating habits are a cornerstone of a happy, healthy, and wealthy retirement journey.

Chapter 13

Secret 13: Regular Health Check-ups and Screenings

Regular health check-ups and screenings are essential components of maintaining good health in retirement. They help in the early detection of health issues, monitoring existing conditions, and ensuring that you stay on track with preventive measures.

Importance of Regular Health Check-ups

1. **Early Detection of Health Issues**: Regular check-ups can help detect potential health problems early, often before symptoms appear. Early detection allows for more effective treatment and better management of health conditions, increasing the chances of a positive outcome.

2. **Monitoring Chronic Conditions**: If you have chronic health conditions such as diabetes, hypertension, or arthritis, regular check-ups are crucial for monitoring your condition and adjusting your treatment plan as needed. This

helps in managing symptoms and preventing complications.

3. **Preventive Care**: Preventive care, including vaccinations and lifestyle counseling, is a key aspect of regular health check-ups. Your healthcare provider can recommend preventive measures tailored to your health status and risk factors, helping you avoid illnesses and maintain overall well-being.

4. **Personalized Health Advice**: Regular visits to your healthcare provider offer an opportunity to receive personalized health advice based on your medical history, lifestyle, and current health status. This can include recommendations for diet, exercise, stress management, and other aspects of a healthy lifestyle.

Essential Health Screenings in Retirement

1. **Blood Pressure Screening**: Regular monitoring of blood pressure is crucial for detecting hypertension, which can lead to serious health issues like heart disease and stroke if left untreated. Aim to have your blood pressure checked at least once a year.

2.   **Cholesterol Check**: High cholesterol levels can increase the risk of heart disease and stroke. It is recommended to have your cholesterol levels checked every 4-6 years, or more frequently if you have risk factors or a history of cardiovascular disease.

3.   **Blood Glucose Testing**: Regular blood glucose testing is important for detecting and managing diabetes. If you are at risk for diabetes or have a family history of the condition, discuss with your doctor how often you should be tested.

4.   **Bone Density Test**: Osteoporosis becomes more common with age, especially in women. A bone density test can help assess your risk of fractures and osteoporosis. Discuss with your healthcare provider when to start screening, typically around age 65.

5.   **Colon Cancer Screening**: Regular screening for colon cancer is recommended starting at age 50, or earlier if you have risk factors such as a family history of the disease. Options include colonoscopy, stool tests, and other methods.

6.   **Mammograms and Pap Smears**: Women should continue to have regular

mammograms to screen for breast cancer, as well as Pap smears and HPV tests for cervical cancer, based on their age and risk factors. Discuss the appropriate screening schedule with your healthcare provider.

7. **Prostate Cancer Screening**: Men should discuss the benefits and risks of prostate cancer screening with their healthcare provider. Screening typically includes a PSA blood test and, if indicated, a digital rectal exam.

8. **Vision and Hearing Tests**: Regular vision and hearing tests are important for detecting changes that could affect your quality of life. Vision tests can identify issues like glaucoma and cataracts, while hearing tests can detect hearing loss.

9. **Skin Checks**: Regular skin checks by a dermatologist can help detect skin cancer early. If you have a history of skin cancer or significant sun exposure, more frequent checks may be recommended.

10. **Dental Check-ups**: Oral health is closely linked to overall health. Regular dental check-ups can prevent and detect issues like gum disease, cavities, and oral cancers.

Tips for Making the Most of Your Health Check-ups

1. **Prepare Ahead**: Before your appointment, make a list of any symptoms, concerns, or questions you have. Bring a list of all medications and supplements you take.

2. **Be Honest and Open**: Provide accurate and complete information about your health, lifestyle, and any changes you've noticed. Honesty with your healthcare provider is key to receiving the best care.

3. **Follow Up**: If your healthcare provider recommends further tests, treatments, or lifestyle changes, make sure to follow through. Schedule follow-up appointments as needed to monitor your progress.

4. **Keep Records**: Maintain a record of your health check-ups, test results, and any treatments you receive. This helps you track your health over time and ensures continuity of care if you see different providers.

5. **Stay Informed**: Stay informed about recommended health screenings and preventive measures for your age group. Being proactive

about your health can help you stay ahead of potential issues.

Investing time in your health today can lead to a happier, healthier tomorrow.

Chapter 14

Secret 14: Mental Health and Wellness

Maintaining mental health and wellness is just as important as physical health, especially in retirement. This period of life can bring about significant changes and adjustments that may lead to stress and anxiety. Focusing on mental well-being through effective stress management and practices like mindfulness and meditation can greatly enhance your quality of life.

Managing Stress and Anxiety

1. **Understand the Sources**: Identify the specific sources of stress and anxiety in your life. Common stressors in retirement include financial concerns, health issues, changes in social dynamics, and adjusting to a new daily routine. Understanding these triggers is the first step towards managing them effectively.
2. **Develop Healthy Coping Mechanisms**: Find healthy ways to cope with stress. This can include physical activity, hobbies, spending time with loved ones, or engaging in creative pursuits. Avoid unhealthy coping mechanisms like

excessive drinking or overeating, which can exacerbate stress.
3. **Stay Connected**: Maintain strong social connections with family, friends, and community groups. Social interaction provides emotional support and can help reduce feelings of loneliness and isolation, which are common contributors to anxiety.
4. **Set Realistic Goals**: Set achievable goals for your daily activities and long-term plans. Having a sense of purpose and accomplishment can reduce stress and provide a positive focus.
5. **Create a Routine**: Establishing a daily routine can provide structure and a sense of normalcy. Include time for relaxation, physical activity, social interactions, and hobbies in your routine.
6. **Seek Professional Help**: If stress and anxiety become overwhelming, consider seeking help from a mental health professional. Therapy, counseling, or medication can be effective in managing more severe cases of anxiety and stress.

Practicing Mindfulness and Meditation

1. **Introduction to Mindfulness**: Mindfulness is the practice of being fully present and engaged in the moment, without judgment. It involves paying

attention to your thoughts, feelings, and sensations in a non-reactive way. Mindfulness can help reduce stress, improve focus, and enhance emotional regulation.
2. **Benefits of Meditation**: Meditation is a practice that involves focusing your mind and eliminating distractions to achieve a state of relaxation and mental clarity. Regular meditation can reduce symptoms of anxiety and depression, improve sleep quality, and increase overall well-being.
3. **Getting Started with Meditation**:
    - **Find a Quiet Space**: Choose a quiet, comfortable space where you can sit or lie down without interruptions.
    - **Set a Time**: Start with just a few minutes a day and gradually increase the duration as you become more comfortable with the practice.
    - **Focus on Your Breath**: Pay attention to your breathing. Inhale deeply and exhale slowly, focusing on the sensation of breath entering and leaving your body.
    - **Use a Mantra or Guided Meditation**: Some people find it helpful to use a mantra (a repeated word or phrase) or follow a guided meditation to keep their mind focused.

4. **Mindfulness Practices**:
    - **Mindful Breathing**: Take a few minutes each day to focus on your breath. Notice the rhythm of your breathing and the sensation of air entering and leaving your body.
    - **Body Scan**: Perform a body scan by mentally scanning each part of your body from head to toe, noticing any sensations or tension and allowing it to release.
    - **Mindful Eating**: Pay full attention to the experience of eating. Notice the taste, texture, and aroma of your food, and eat slowly and deliberately.
    - **Mindful Walking**: Take a walk and focus on the sensation of each step, the feeling of the ground beneath your feet, and the sights and sounds around you.
5. **Incorporate Mindfulness into Daily Life**: Integrate mindfulness practices into your daily routine. This can include mindful moments during daily activities like brushing your teeth, washing dishes, or waiting in line. The goal is to be fully present and engaged in whatever you are doing.

6. **Join a Group or Class**: Consider joining a mindfulness or meditation group or taking a class. This can provide guidance, support, and a sense of community, which can enhance your practice.
7. **Use Technology**: There are numerous apps and online resources available to help you practice mindfulness and meditation. These can provide guided sessions, timers, and tracking tools to support your journey.
8. **Be Patient and Consistent**: Developing a mindfulness or meditation practice takes time and consistency. Be patient with yourself and make it a regular part of your routine. The benefits will increase with continued practice.

These practices provide valuable tools to navigate the changes and challenges of retirement, helping you to enjoy a more balanced, peaceful, and fulfilling life.

Chapter 15

Secret 15: Adopting a Healthy Sleep Routine

Quality sleep is a cornerstone of good health and well-being, especially in retirement. A healthy sleep routine can improve your physical health, mental clarity, mood, and overall quality of life. This section delves into the importance of sleep and offers practical tips for achieving better sleep.

Importance of Sleep

1. **Physical Health**: Adequate sleep is vital for physical health. It helps the body repair and regenerate tissues, build muscle, and support the immune system. Poor sleep is linked to an increased risk of chronic conditions such as heart disease, diabetes, obesity, and hypertension.

2. **Mental Health**: Sleep plays a crucial role in cognitive function, including memory, attention, and decision-making. Good sleep can enhance creativity and problem-solving skills. Conversely, sleep deprivation is associated with

cognitive decline and increased risk of mental health issues like depression and anxiety.

3. **Emotional Well-being**: Quality sleep contributes to emotional stability and resilience. It helps regulate mood and reduce irritability and stress. People who get enough sleep are better equipped to handle daily challenges and maintain a positive outlook.

4. **Longevity**: Research indicates that consistent, adequate sleep is associated with a longer lifespan. Sleep helps maintain overall health, reducing the risk of life-shortening diseases and conditions.

Tips for Better Sleep

1. **Establish a Regular Sleep Schedule**: Go to bed and wake up at the same time every day, even on weekends. Consistency helps regulate your body's internal clock, making it easier to fall asleep and wake up naturally.

2. **Create a Restful Environment**:
    - **Comfortable Bed**: Ensure your mattress and pillows are comfortable and supportive.

- **Dark Room**: Use blackout curtains or an eye mask to keep the room dark.
- **Cool Temperature**: Keep the bedroom cool, around 60-67°F (15-19°C).
- **Quiet Space**: Use earplugs or a white noise machine to block out disruptive noises.

3. **Limit Exposure to Screens**: Reduce screen time from TVs, computers, tablets, and smartphones at least an hour before bed. The blue light emitted by screens can interfere with the production of melatonin, the hormone that regulates sleep.

4. **Develop a Bedtime Routine**: Establish a calming pre-sleep routine to signal to your body that it's time to wind down. This could include reading, taking a warm bath, listening to soothing music, or practicing relaxation techniques like deep breathing or meditation.

5. **Watch Your Diet**: Avoid large meals, caffeine, and alcohol close to bedtime. Caffeine and nicotine are stimulants that can disrupt sleep, while heavy meals can cause discomfort. Alcohol might make you feel sleepy initially but can disrupt sleep later in the night.

6. **Stay Physically Active**: Regular physical activity can help you fall asleep faster and enjoy deeper sleep. However, avoid vigorous exercise close to bedtime, as it may be too stimulating.

7. **Manage Stress and Anxiety**: Practice stress-reducing techniques such as mindfulness, meditation, or yoga. Keeping a journal to jot down your thoughts before bed can help clear your mind and reduce anxiety.

8. **Limit Naps**: While naps can be beneficial, especially if you didn't sleep well the night before, limit them to 20-30 minutes and avoid napping late in the day to prevent interference with nighttime sleep.

9. **Avoid Stimulants**: Refrain from consuming stimulants like caffeine and nicotine in the hours leading up to bedtime, as they can interfere with your ability to fall asleep and stay asleep.

10. **Use Sleep Aids Sparingly**: While over-the-counter sleep aids and prescription medications can be helpful for occasional use, they should not be relied upon long-term. Consult with a healthcare provider if you are experiencing chronic sleep problems.

11. **Get Exposure to Natural Light**: Spend time outdoors in natural sunlight during the day. Exposure to natural light helps regulate your sleep-wake cycle and improve sleep quality.

12. **Keep a Sleep Diary**: Track your sleep patterns, daily habits, and any factors that might be affecting your sleep. This can help you identify patterns and make necessary adjustments to improve your sleep quality.

13. **Seek Professional Help**: If you continue to have trouble sleeping despite making these changes, consider consulting a sleep specialist or healthcare provider. Sleep disorders like insomnia, sleep apnea, or restless legs syndrome may require professional intervention.

A healthy sleep routine will provide the energy, mental clarity, and emotional balance needed to fully enjoy this stage of life.

Part 4

Staying Engaged and Happy

Chapter 16

Secret 16: Finding a Purpose

Retirement is a time of great opportunity to explore new interests and discover what truly brings you joy and fulfillment. Finding a sense of purpose can significantly enhance your happiness and overall well-being. Whether through discovering new passions, volunteering, or engaging in community service, staying active and purposeful is key to a rewarding retirement.

Discovering New Passions

1. **Reflect on Your Interests**: Take time to reflect on activities and hobbies that have always interested you but that you might not have had time to pursue during your working years. This can be anything from gardening to painting, learning a musical instrument, or taking up a new sport.

2. **Try New Activities**: Don't be afraid to step out of your comfort zone and try something completely new. Join a club, take a class, or attend workshops to explore different interests.

Many community centers and local organizations offer a variety of programs tailored for retirees.

3.   **Lifelong Learning**: Engaging in lifelong learning can be incredibly fulfilling. Enroll in courses at local colleges or universities, either in person or online, to learn about subjects that fascinate you. This not only keeps your mind sharp but also provides a sense of accomplishment and purpose.

4.   **Travel and Explore**: If you have a passion for travel, use retirement as an opportunity to explore new places and cultures. Traveling can broaden your horizons, introduce you to new people, and create memorable experiences that enrich your life.

5.   **Pursue Creative Outlets**: Creativity can be a powerful way to find purpose. Whether it's writing, painting, crafting, or photography, creative pursuits allow you to express yourself and create something meaningful.

Volunteering and Community Service

1.   **Identify Causes You Care About**: Think about the issues and causes that are important to you. Whether it's animal welfare, environmental

conservation, education, or healthcare, there are countless organizations that would value your time and skills.

2. **Research Volunteer Opportunities**: Look for volunteer opportunities that align with your interests and skills. Many organizations, from local nonprofits to national charities, need volunteers. Websites like VolunteerMatch can help you find opportunities in your area.

3. **Leverage Your Skills and Experience**: Your professional skills and experience can be incredibly valuable in a volunteer setting. Consider mentoring young professionals, offering pro bono consulting, or providing administrative support to a nonprofit organization.

4. **Join Community Groups**: Engaging with community groups, such as neighborhood associations, religious groups, or hobby clubs, can provide a sense of belonging and purpose. These groups often have volunteer opportunities and events that allow you to contribute to your community.

5. **Mentorship and Tutoring**: Sharing your knowledge and experience with others through mentorship or tutoring can be incredibly

rewarding. Many schools, community centers, and nonprofit organizations seek volunteers to support students and young professionals.

6. **Start Your Own Initiative**: If you see a need in your community that isn't being addressed, consider starting your own initiative or nonprofit. This could be anything from organizing a local clean-up to creating a support group for retirees.

7. **Social Engagement**: Volunteering is also a great way to meet new people and build social connections. The camaraderie and sense of community that come from working together towards a common goal can enhance your social life and overall happiness.

8. **Commit to Regular Involvement**: To truly find purpose in volunteering, commit to regular involvement. Whether it's weekly, monthly, or seasonally, consistent participation helps build deeper connections and a stronger sense of accomplishment.

Additional Tips for Finding Purpose

1. **Set Personal Goals**: Set personal goals related to your new passions and volunteer

activities. Having specific, achievable goals provides a sense of direction and purpose.

2. **Balance Your Time**: While finding purpose is important, it's also crucial to balance your time. Ensure you have enough time for relaxation, self-care, and spending with loved ones.

3. **Stay Open to Change**: Your interests and passions may evolve over time. Stay open to new opportunities and be willing to adjust your pursuits as needed.

4. **Celebrate Your Contributions**: Recognize and celebrate the impact of your contributions, whether in your personal pursuits or volunteer work. Acknowledging your efforts reinforces the value of what you are doing and boosts your sense of purpose.

By discovering new passions and engaging in volunteering and community service, you can find a deep sense of purpose and fulfillment in retirement. Staying active and involved not only enhances your happiness but also positively impacts your community and enriches your life in meaningful ways.

Chapter 17

Secret 17: Building and Maintaining Relationships

Strong relationships are a cornerstone of happiness and well-being in retirement. Staying connected with family and friends, as well as meeting new people, can provide emotional support, reduce feelings of loneliness, and add richness to your life. This section explores the importance of nurturing existing relationships and tips for expanding your social circle.

Staying Connected with Family and Friends

1. **Regular Communication**: Make it a habit to regularly communicate with family and friends. This can be through phone calls, video chats, emails, or social media. Staying in touch keeps relationships strong and shows your loved ones that you care.

2. **Family Gatherings**: Organize family gatherings or get-togethers. Whether it's a weekly dinner, a monthly brunch, or an annual family

reunion, spending time together helps maintain close bonds.

3. **Shared Activities**: Engage in activities that you and your loved ones enjoy. This could include hobbies like gardening, cooking, hiking, or playing games. Shared experiences create lasting memories and strengthen connections.

4. **Supportive Role**: Be a supportive presence in your loved ones' lives. Offer help when needed, listen actively, and provide encouragement. Being there for each other through life's ups and downs is vital for maintaining strong relationships.

5. **Celebrate Milestones**: Acknowledge and celebrate important milestones such as birthdays, anniversaries, and achievements. Celebrating together strengthens the sense of belonging and appreciation.

6. **Plan Visits and Trips**: If family and friends live far away, plan visits or trips to see them. Traveling to visit loved ones shows that you value the relationship and are willing to make the effort to stay connected.

7. **Use Technology**: Leverage technology to stay connected, especially if distance is a barrier. Video calls, group chats, and social media platforms can help bridge the gap and keep relationships strong.

Meeting New People

1. **Join Clubs and Groups**: Participate in clubs and groups that align with your interests. This could be a book club, gardening group, sports team, or hobby class. Joining these groups provides opportunities to meet like-minded people and form new friendships.

2. **Attend Community Events**: Get involved in community events such as festivals, fairs, and local gatherings. These events offer a chance to socialize, meet new people, and feel more connected to your community.

3. **Volunteer**: Volunteering is not only a great way to give back but also an excellent opportunity to meet new people. Working together towards a common goal fosters camaraderie and can lead to meaningful relationships.

4. **Take Classes**: Enroll in classes or workshops to learn something new. Whether it's art, music, cooking, or fitness, classes provide a structured environment for meeting people with similar interests.

5. **Social Media and Online Communities**: Use social media and online communities to connect with others. Join groups and forums related to your interests, participate in discussions, and build relationships with people from different parts of the world.

6. **Attend Religious or Spiritual Gatherings**: If you are religious or spiritual, attending services or gatherings at your place of worship can be a great way to meet new people and build a supportive community.

7. **Network Through Friends**: Expand your social circle by networking through existing friends. Attend parties, social gatherings, or events where you can meet friends of friends and build new connections.

8. **Be Open and Approachable**: Make an effort to be open and approachable when meeting new people. Smile, make eye contact, and show genuine interest in getting to know others.

Positive body language and a friendly demeanor can make a big difference.

9. **Host Social Gatherings**: Host social gatherings at your home or in your community. Invite neighbors, friends, and acquaintances to foster a sense of community and create opportunities for new friendships.

10. **Practice Active Listening**: When meeting new people, practice active listening. Pay attention to what they say, ask questions, and show empathy. Building strong relationships starts with making others feel valued and heard.

Additional Tips for Building and Maintaining Relationships

1. **Be Genuine and Authentic**: Authenticity is key to building meaningful relationships. Be yourself, share your true thoughts and feelings, and encourage others to do the same.

2. **Show Appreciation**: Regularly express gratitude and appreciation to your loved ones and new friends. A simple thank you or a kind gesture can go a long way in strengthening bonds.

3. **Resolve Conflicts Constructively**: Address conflicts or misunderstandings calmly and constructively. Effective communication and willingness to find solutions help maintain healthy relationships.

4. **Balance Giving and Receiving**: Strive for a balance between giving and receiving in relationships. Offer support and help when needed, but also be open to receiving support from others.

5. **Prioritize Relationships**: Make relationships a priority in your life. Dedicate time and effort to nurturing connections, and don't let busy schedules or other commitments take precedence over your social well-being.

Strong relationships provide emotional support, reduce feelings of isolation, and contribute significantly to your happiness and well-being.

Chapter 18

Secret 18: Traveling and Exploring New Places

Traveling and exploring new places can be one of the most rewarding experiences during retirement. It offers a sense of adventure, the opportunity to learn about different cultures, and a chance to create lasting memories. This section delves into the benefits of travel in retirement and provides tips for planning budget-friendly trips.

Benefits of Travel in Retirement

1. **Mental Stimulation**: Traveling to new places stimulates the brain, exposing you to different environments, languages, and cultures. This mental stimulation can help keep your mind sharp, improve cognitive function, and even delay the onset of dementia.

2. **Physical Activity**: Travel often involves physical activities such as walking, hiking, and sightseeing, which contribute to better physical health. Regular physical activity helps maintain

mobility, reduces the risk of chronic diseases, and enhances overall well-being.

3. **Emotional Well-being**: Exploring new places and experiencing different cultures can enhance your emotional well-being. Travel provides a break from routine, reduces stress, and promotes relaxation and happiness. The excitement and joy of discovering new destinations can boost your mood and create a sense of fulfillment.

4. **Social Connections**: Traveling allows you to meet new people and make friends from different backgrounds. Whether you join group tours, participate in local events, or stay in social accommodations like hostels, travel can expand your social network and enhance your sense of community.

5. **Cultural Enrichment**: Exposure to different cultures broadens your perspective and deepens your understanding of the world. Visiting historical sites, museums, and cultural landmarks enriches your knowledge and appreciation of diverse traditions, customs, and histories.

6. **Personal Growth**: Travel encourages personal growth by pushing you out of your comfort zone and presenting new challenges. Navigating unfamiliar places, trying new foods, and adapting to different environments fosters resilience, adaptability, and confidence.

7. **Quality Time with Loved Ones**: Traveling with family or friends provides an opportunity to strengthen relationships and create cherished memories. Shared travel experiences build bonds and offer a unique way to spend quality time together.

Planning Budget-Friendly Trips

1. **Set a Travel Budget**: Start by setting a realistic travel budget based on your financial situation. Determine how much you can afford to spend on transportation, accommodation, food, activities, and souvenirs. Sticking to a budget helps ensure that you enjoy your travels without financial stress.

2. **Travel Off-Peak**: Plan your trips during off-peak seasons when prices for flights, accommodations, and attractions are lower. Avoiding peak travel times can save you money

and provide a more relaxed and enjoyable experience without the crowds.

3. **Look for Deals and Discounts**: Take advantage of travel deals, discounts, and promotions. Sign up for newsletters from airlines, travel agencies, and deal websites to stay informed about special offers. Consider using senior discounts available for transportation, accommodations, and attractions.

4. **Use Reward Points and Miles**: If you have accumulated reward points or frequent flier miles, use them to reduce travel costs. Many credit card companies offer travel rewards that can be redeemed for flights, hotel stays, and other travel expenses.

5. **Choose Budget-Friendly Destinations**: Select destinations that offer good value for your money. Some countries and cities are more affordable than others, especially when it comes to accommodation, food, and activities. Research destinations with a lower cost of living to stretch your travel budget further.

6. **Stay in Affordable Accommodations**: Consider staying in budget-friendly accommodations such as hostels, guesthouses,

vacation rentals, or Airbnb. Booking a place with a kitchen allows you to prepare your own meals, saving money on dining out.

7. **Travel Light**: Pack efficiently to avoid extra baggage fees and make your travels more convenient. Bring versatile clothing and essentials, and avoid overpacking. Traveling light can also make it easier to use public transportation and move around more freely.

8. **Use Public Transportation**: Public transportation is often more affordable than taxis or rental cars. Research the public transportation options available at your destination, such as buses, trains, and subways, to get around cost-effectively.

9. **Plan and Book in Advance**: Planning and booking your trip in advance can help you secure better deals on flights, accommodations, and activities. Early booking often comes with discounts and allows you to choose from a wider range of options.

10. **Eat Like a Local**: Save money on food by dining at local eateries, street food vendors, and markets instead of expensive restaurants. Eating

like a local not only reduces costs but also provides an authentic culinary experience.

11. **Free and Low-Cost Activities**: Research free and low-cost activities at your destination. Many cities offer free walking tours, museums with free entry days, and outdoor attractions such as parks and beaches. Look for events and festivals that don't charge an entrance fee.

12. **Travel Insurance**: While it may seem like an additional expense, travel insurance can save you money in the long run by covering unexpected costs such as medical emergencies, trip cancellations, and lost luggage.

Additional Tips for Enjoying Travel in Retirement

1. **Plan Flexibly**: While it's good to have an itinerary, leave room for spontaneity. Sometimes the best experiences come from unplanned adventures.

2. **Health Precautions**: Take necessary health precautions, especially if traveling abroad. Ensure you have any required vaccinations, bring essential medications, and stay informed about the health conditions at your destination.

3. **Learn Basic Phrases**: If traveling to a non-English-speaking country, learn a few basic phrases in the local language. It helps in communication and shows respect for the local culture.

4. **Document Your Journey**: Keep a travel journal or blog to document your experiences. Taking photos and writing about your travels can help you cherish memories and share your adventures with family and friends.

5. **Stay Open-Minded**: Embrace new experiences and stay open-minded. Every destination has something unique to offer, and being receptive to different cultures and lifestyles can enrich your travel experience.

Traveling and exploring new places can significantly enhance your retirement years, providing adventure, learning, and personal growth. By planning budget-friendly trips and staying open to new experiences, you can enjoy the many benefits that travel brings without straining your finances.

Chapter 19

Secret 19: Lifelong Learning

Retirement is an excellent time to embrace lifelong learning, keeping your mind sharp and engaged. Taking up new hobbies and interests, and enrolling in courses and workshops, can greatly enhance your quality of life, provide personal fulfillment, and offer numerous mental health benefits. This section explores the advantages of lifelong learning and offers practical advice on how to integrate continuous education into your retirement.

Taking Up New Hobbies and Interests

1. **Personal Fulfillment**: Discovering new hobbies and interests can provide immense personal satisfaction and a sense of achievement. Whether you've always wanted to paint, garden, play an instrument, or write, now is the perfect time to explore these passions.

2. **Mental Stimulation**: Engaging in new activities keeps your brain active and challenged. Learning new skills and hobbies can improve cognitive function, enhance memory, and increase overall mental sharpness.

3. **Social Interaction**: Many hobbies offer opportunities for social interaction. Joining a book club, a gardening group, or an art class can help you meet like-minded individuals, fostering social connections and reducing feelings of isolation.

4. **Physical Health**: Certain hobbies, such as gardening, dancing, or hiking, provide physical activity, which is crucial for maintaining good health in retirement. Staying physically active through enjoyable hobbies can improve mobility, balance, and overall well-being.

5. **Stress Relief**: Hobbies can serve as a great stress reliever. Activities such as knitting, painting, or playing music can provide a calming effect, helping to reduce anxiety and promote relaxation.

6. **Creativity and Innovation**: Taking up new hobbies can enhance your creativity and innovative thinking. Creative activities stimulate different areas of the brain and can lead to new ways of thinking and problem-solving.

Enrolling in Courses and Workshops

1. **Lifelong Learning Opportunities**: Many educational institutions and community centers offer courses and workshops designed for retirees. These can range from academic subjects to practical skills, providing a structured way to continue learning.

2. **Online Courses**: The internet offers a wealth of online courses on virtually any subject. Websites like Coursera, Udemy, and Khan Academy provide access to courses taught by experts from around the world, allowing you to learn at your own pace from the comfort of your home.

3. **Community College Classes**: Local community colleges often offer classes for seniors at reduced rates. These classes cover a wide range of subjects, including art, history, technology, and health, providing opportunities to learn new skills and meet new people.

4. **Workshops and Seminars**: Attend workshops and seminars on topics that interest you. These can be found through local libraries, community centers, and professional organizations. Workshops provide hands-on

learning experiences and are often more interactive than traditional classes.

5. **Guest Lectures and Events**: Many universities and cultural institutions host guest lectures and events open to the public. These events can be a great way to learn from experts in various fields and stay informed about current topics and trends.

6. **Language Learning**: Learning a new language can be a particularly rewarding challenge. Language classes, whether in-person or online, not only improve cognitive function but also open up new travel opportunities and cultural experiences.

7. **Professional Development**: If you have a specific professional interest or want to stay connected to your career field, consider enrolling in courses that offer professional development. Many industries offer continuing education credits that can keep your skills current.

Tips for Embracing Lifelong Learning

1. **Identify Your Interests**: Start by identifying subjects or activities you are passionate about. Consider what you've always

wanted to learn or try but never had the time to pursue.

2. **Set Goals**: Set realistic and achievable goals for your learning journey. Having specific objectives helps keep you motivated and provides a sense of direction.

3. **Create a Learning Schedule**: Allocate regular time in your schedule for learning. Consistency is key to making progress and maintaining a lifelong learning habit.

4. **Stay Curious**: Cultivate a mindset of curiosity and openness. Be willing to explore new topics and step out of your comfort zone. Curiosity drives learning and keeps the process exciting.

5. **Leverage Technology**: Utilize technology to access learning resources. Online courses, educational apps, and virtual libraries can provide a vast array of information and tools to support your learning goals.

6. **Join Learning Communities**: Engage with communities of learners who share your interests. Online forums, social media groups, and local clubs can provide support,

encouragement, and opportunities for discussion and collaboration.

7. **Reflect and Adjust**: Periodically reflect on your learning experiences and adjust your goals and methods as needed. Flexibility allows you to adapt your learning journey to fit your evolving interests and needs.

Chapter 20

Secret 20: Giving Back to the Community

Volunteering and engaging in community service during retirement can be incredibly fulfilling. It provides a sense of purpose, builds social connections, and significantly enhances your overall happiness.

Volunteering Opportunities

1. **Local Charities and Nonprofits**: Many local charities and nonprofit organizations are always in need of volunteers. Whether it's helping at a food bank, animal shelter, or community center, there are countless ways to get involved and make a difference.

2. **Educational Institutions**: Schools and educational programs often seek volunteers to assist with tutoring, mentoring, and administrative tasks. Sharing your knowledge and experience with students can be incredibly rewarding.

3. **Healthcare Facilities**: Hospitals, clinics, and nursing homes often have volunteer programs. Volunteers can provide companionship to patients, assist with activities, or help with administrative work.

4. **Environmental Organizations**: If you're passionate about the environment, consider volunteering with organizations dedicated to conservation, clean-up efforts, and sustainability projects. Activities might include planting trees, cleaning up beaches, or participating in wildlife conservation.

5. **Religious and Spiritual Organizations**: Many religious institutions have outreach programs that rely on volunteers. These programs often include community outreach, support services, and event planning.

6. **Community Events**: Volunteering at local events, such as festivals, fairs, and charity runs, is a great way to meet new people and contribute to your community's vibrancy.

7. **Online Volunteering**: If mobility is an issue or you prefer remote opportunities, many organizations offer virtual volunteer roles. This can include tutoring, administrative support,

social media management, or providing companionship through phone calls or video chats.

8. **Youth Programs**: Volunteering with youth organizations like the Boy Scouts, Girl Scouts, or local sports teams allows you to mentor and positively influence the younger generation.

9. **Arts and Culture**: Museums, theaters, and cultural organizations often need volunteers to help with tours, events, and administrative tasks. This is a great way to support the arts and engage with your community's cultural heritage.

10. **Political and Advocacy Groups**: If you're passionate about a particular cause, consider volunteering with political campaigns or advocacy groups. This can involve organizing events, canvassing, or providing administrative support.

Impact of Community Service on Happiness

1. **Sense of Purpose**: Volunteering provides a sense of purpose and fulfillment. Knowing that your efforts are making a difference in the lives

of others can bring immense satisfaction and meaning to your life.

2. **Social Connections**: Community service offers opportunities to meet new people and build meaningful relationships. Volunteering with others fosters a sense of camaraderie and belonging, reducing feelings of isolation and loneliness.

3. **Increased Happiness**: Studies have shown that volunteering can boost happiness and life satisfaction. Helping others releases endorphins, also known as "helper's high," which can improve your mood and overall well-being.

4. **Enhanced Self-Esteem**: Contributing to the community and receiving appreciation and gratitude can enhance your self-esteem and confidence. It reinforces your sense of worth and capability.

5. **Stress Reduction**: Engaging in volunteer work can be a great way to reduce stress. The act of giving back and focusing on others helps shift your perspective and can provide a break from your own worries and concerns.

6. **Learning and Growth**: Volunteering exposes you to new experiences and challenges, promoting continuous learning and personal growth. It can also provide opportunities to develop new skills and discover new interests.

7. **Physical Health Benefits**: Many volunteer activities involve physical tasks that can help you stay active. Additionally, the mental health benefits of volunteering, such as reduced stress and increased happiness, can contribute to better overall health.

8. **Community Improvement**: By volunteering, you play a direct role in improving your community. This can create a more positive and supportive environment for everyone, including yourself.

9. **Legacy Building**: Volunteering allows you to leave a lasting impact on your community. Whether through direct service or mentoring others, your contributions can have a ripple effect, inspiring future generations to give back as well.

10. **Expanded Perspectives**: Community service exposes you to different perspectives and life experiences. This can foster empathy,

compassion, and a deeper understanding of the diverse needs within your community.

Additional Tips for Volunteering

1. **Choose What Resonates**: Select volunteer opportunities that align with your passions and interests. When you care deeply about the cause, the experience will be more meaningful and enjoyable.

2. **Start Small**: If you're new to volunteering, start with small commitments and gradually take on more as you become comfortable. This prevents burnout and allows you to find the right fit.

3. **Be Consistent**: Regular volunteering, even in small amounts, can be more impactful than sporadic efforts. Consistency helps build stronger relationships and ensures that your contributions have a lasting effect.

4. **Bring Friends or Family**: Volunteering can be a wonderful activity to share with friends or family members. It strengthens bonds and makes the experience more enjoyable.

5. **Stay Flexible**: Be open to different types of volunteer work. Sometimes, the most fulfilling opportunities are those you didn't initially consider.

6. **Reflect on Your Experiences**: Take time to reflect on your volunteer experiences and how they've impacted you. This can deepen your sense of fulfillment and help you identify the most rewarding aspects of giving back.

Part 5:

Personal Growth and Fulfillment

Chapter 21

Secret 21: Practicing Gratitude

Embracing gratitude in your daily life can profoundly impact your well-being and overall outlook during retirement. Gratitude enhances your mental health, fosters positivity, and can even improve your physical health. This section explores the importance of gratitude and provides practical advice on how to keep a gratitude journal.

Importance of Gratitude

1. **Enhances Mental Health**: Practicing gratitude has been shown to reduce symptoms of depression and anxiety. Focusing on the positive aspects of your life helps shift your perspective from what's lacking to what's abundant, promoting a more optimistic mindset.

2. **Increases Happiness**: Regularly expressing gratitude can significantly boost your overall happiness. Recognizing and appreciating the good things in your life creates positive emotions, making you feel more content and fulfilled.

3. **Improves Relationships**: Expressing gratitude to others strengthens relationships. Acknowledging the kindness and support of friends and family fosters deeper connections and encourages a supportive and loving environment.

4. **Boosts Resilience**: Gratitude helps build emotional resilience. By focusing on the positive aspects of life, you become better equipped to handle challenges and setbacks, maintaining a sense of hope and determination.

5. **Enhances Physical Health**: Studies have shown that grateful people tend to have better physical health. Practicing gratitude can lead to better sleep, lower blood pressure, and a stronger immune system, contributing to overall well-being.

6. **Reduces Stress**: Focusing on what you are grateful for can reduce stress levels. Gratitude shifts your focus away from worries and negative thoughts, promoting a more relaxed and peaceful state of mind.

7. **Increases Self-Esteem**: Recognizing your own achievements and the positive aspects of your life can boost your self-esteem. Gratitude

helps you appreciate your worth and the value you bring to the world.

Keeping a Gratitude Journal

1. **Choose a Journal**: Select a journal that you find visually appealing and comfortable to write in. It can be a simple notebook, a fancy diary, or even a digital app designed for journaling.

2. **Set a Regular Time**: Establish a routine for writing in your gratitude journal. This could be in the morning to start your day positively or in the evening to reflect on the day's events. Consistency is key to making it a habit.

3. **Start with Three Things**: Begin by writing down three things you are grateful for each day. These can be small or significant, ranging from a delicious meal to a meaningful conversation or a beautiful sunset.

4. **Be Specific**: When listing what you're grateful for, be as specific as possible. Instead of writing, "I'm grateful for my family," you could write, "I'm grateful for the fun game night I had with my family." Specific details make the gratitude more tangible and meaningful.

5. **Reflect on Positive Experiences**: Use your journal to reflect on positive experiences and moments of joy. Reliving these moments through writing can enhance your sense of gratitude and prolong the positive feelings associated with them.

6. **Express Gratitude for Challenges**: Try to find aspects to be grateful for even in challenging situations. This could be lessons learned, personal growth, or the support you received during tough times. Gratitude in adversity builds resilience and perspective.

7. **Include People**: Acknowledge the people who bring joy and support to your life. Expressing gratitude for their presence and actions strengthens your relationships and fosters a sense of connection.

8. **Write Letters of Gratitude**: Occasionally, write a letter of gratitude to someone who has positively impacted your life. Even if you don't send it, the act of writing can deepen your feelings of appreciation.

9. **Stay Positive and Honest**: Focus on positive and genuine expressions of gratitude. Avoid forcing yourself to write things you don't

truly feel grateful for, as authenticity is crucial for the practice to be effective.

10. **Review Your Entries**: Periodically review your past entries. This practice can remind you of the many good things in your life, reinforcing positive feelings and helping you maintain a grateful mindset.

Additional Tips for Practicing Gratitude

1. **Share Your Gratitude**: Share what you're grateful for with others. This can be done during conversations, in thank-you notes, or through social media. Sharing gratitude spreads positivity and can inspire others to practice gratitude as well.

2. **Mindfulness and Meditation**: Incorporate mindfulness and meditation practices focused on gratitude. Taking a few moments each day to meditate on what you're grateful for can enhance your overall sense of appreciation.

3. **Gratitude Jar**: Create a gratitude jar where you and your family members can add notes of things you're grateful for. Reading these notes together can be a heartwarming and bonding experience.

4. **Daily Affirmations**: Start your day with positive affirmations that include expressions of gratitude. Affirmations set a positive tone for the day and reinforce a grateful mindset.

5. **Visual Reminders**: Place visual reminders of things you're grateful for around your home. Photos, quotes, or mementos can serve as constant prompts to focus on the positive aspects of your life.

Chapter 22

Secret 22: Embracing Change and Adaptability

Retirement brings significant life changes, and your ability to embrace these changes and remain adaptable is crucial for maintaining happiness and fulfillment. Learning how to deal with life changes and staying flexible and open-minded can enhance your overall well-being and make your retirement years more rewarding. This section explores strategies for dealing with life changes and the importance of maintaining a flexible and open-minded attitude.

Dealing with Life Changes

1. **Accepting Change as a Natural Part of Life**: Change is inevitable and a natural part of life. Recognizing and accepting this can help you approach changes with a positive mindset. Viewing change as an opportunity for growth rather than a disruption can transform your experience.

2. **Managing Expectations**: Retirement often brings shifts in daily routines, social circles,

and personal identity. Managing your expectations and being realistic about the changes you'll face can help you navigate this transition more smoothly.

3.   **Seeking Support**: Don't hesitate to seek support from friends, family, or professional counselors. Talking about your feelings and experiences can provide comfort and perspective, making it easier to adapt to new circumstances.

4.   **Staying Connected**: Maintaining strong social connections is vital during times of change. Stay in touch with old friends and make an effort to build new relationships. A robust support network can provide stability and encouragement.

5.   **Focusing on Self-Care**: Prioritize self-care to maintain your physical and mental health. Exercise regularly, eat well, get enough sleep, and engage in activities that bring you joy and relaxation. Taking care of yourself helps you stay resilient in the face of change.

6.   **Developing a Routine**: Establishing a new daily routine can provide a sense of structure and purpose. While it's important to stay flexible,

having some consistency in your days can help you feel more grounded during transitions.

7. **Setting New Goals**: Retirement is an excellent time to set new goals and pursue interests you've always wanted to explore. Setting goals gives you a sense of direction and motivation, helping you adapt to your new lifestyle.

8. **Learning New Skills**: Embrace the opportunity to learn new skills or hobbies. Whether it's taking up a new sport, learning a language, or mastering a craft, acquiring new skills keeps your mind engaged and adaptable.

9. **Practicing Patience**: Adjusting to significant changes takes time. Be patient with yourself as you navigate this new phase of life. Allow yourself to gradually adapt and find your new rhythm.

Staying Flexible and Open-Minded

1. **Adopting a Growth Mindset**: A growth mindset, the belief that you can learn and grow throughout your life, is crucial for adaptability. Embrace challenges as opportunities to learn and develop new strengths.

2. **Being Open to New Experiences**: Try to stay open to new experiences and opportunities. Whether it's traveling to a new destination, trying a new activity, or meeting new people, being open-minded enriches your life and enhances your adaptability.

3. **Practicing Mindfulness**: Mindfulness practices, such as meditation and deep breathing, can help you stay present and grounded. These practices improve your ability to manage stress and adapt to change with a calm and centered approach.

4. **Remaining Positive**: Maintain a positive attitude towards change. Focus on the potential benefits and new opportunities that changes can bring. Positivity makes it easier to navigate transitions and find joy in new experiences.

5. **Seeking Continuous Learning**: Commit to lifelong learning. Stay curious and seek knowledge in various fields. Continuous learning keeps your mind sharp and flexible, enabling you to adapt more easily to new situations.

6. **Being Resourceful**: Cultivate resourcefulness by finding creative solutions to challenges. Resourcefulness involves using your

skills and knowledge to navigate new circumstances effectively.

7. **Letting Go of the Past**: While it's important to cherish your memories, clinging to the past can hinder your ability to embrace the present and future. Practice letting go of what no longer serves you and focus on creating new, fulfilling experiences.

8. **Adapting Your Plans**: Be willing to adjust your plans as needed. Life is unpredictable, and flexibility allows you to adapt to unforeseen changes without feeling overwhelmed.

9. **Cultivating Resilience**: Build resilience by developing coping strategies and a strong support network. Resilience helps you bounce back from setbacks and maintain a positive outlook during challenging times.

Chapter 23

Secret 23: Simplifying Your Life

Simplifying your life during retirement can lead to greater peace of mind, increased happiness, and a stronger focus on what truly matters. Decluttering and downsizing your living space and lifestyle can help eliminate unnecessary stress and create a more manageable and fulfilling environment.

Decluttering and Downsizing

1. **Benefits of Decluttering**:
    - **Reduces Stress**: A cluttered environment can contribute to stress and anxiety. Decluttering helps create a more organized and serene living space, promoting relaxation and mental clarity.
    - **Increases Efficiency**: When your belongings are well-organized, it's easier to find what you need, saving time and reducing frustration.
    - **Enhances Well-Being**: A clean and tidy environment can boost your mood and overall well-being. Living in an

uncluttered space allows you to feel more in control and at peace.

2. **Steps to Declutter**:

    o **Start Small**: Begin with one room or area at a time. Trying to declutter your entire home at once can be overwhelming. Start with a small, manageable space, such as a closet or a drawer.
    o **Sort Items**: Sort your belongings into categories: keep, donate, sell, and discard. Be honest with yourself about what you truly need and use.
    o **Let Go of Sentimental Items**: While it's important to cherish memories, holding onto too many sentimental items can lead to clutter. Select a few meaningful pieces to keep and consider taking photos of the rest to preserve the memories without the physical clutter.
    o **Create a System**: Develop an organizational system that works for you. Use storage bins, shelves, and labels to keep items in order and easily accessible.

3. **Benefits of Downsizing**:

- **Financial Savings**: Downsizing to a smaller home can significantly reduce expenses such as mortgage payments, property taxes, utilities, and maintenance costs.
- **Easier Maintenance**: A smaller home is easier to clean and maintain, allowing you to spend less time on chores and more time on activities you enjoy.
- **More Mobility**: Downsizing can make it easier to move or travel. With fewer belongings and a smaller home, relocating or taking extended trips becomes more manageable.

4. **Steps to Downsize**:

   - **Assess Your Needs**: Consider your current and future needs when deciding on the size and type of home you want. Think about factors such as mobility, proximity to family and amenities, and the amount of space you truly need.
   - **Plan the Move**: Once you've decided to downsize, create a plan for the move. Determine what items will fit in your new space and what you can sell, donate, or discard.

- **Organize a Sale**: Selling unwanted items can provide extra funds for your move. Organize a garage sale or use online platforms to sell furniture, appliances, and other items you no longer need.
- **Embrace Minimalism**: Adopt a minimalist mindset by focusing on owning fewer, high-quality items that serve a purpose or bring you joy. This approach can help you maintain a simpler, clutter-free lifestyle in your new home.

Focusing on What Truly Matters

1. **Identify Your Priorities**:

   - **Reflect on Values**: Take time to reflect on your core values and what truly matters to you. This can include relationships, health, personal growth, and hobbies. Knowing your values helps you prioritize activities and commitments that align with your true self.
   - **Set Goals**: Establish clear goals based on your values. These goals can guide your daily actions and decisions, ensuring you focus on what brings you fulfillment and joy.

2. **Simplify Commitments**:

    o **Evaluate Obligations**: Assess your current commitments and determine which ones are essential and which can be let go. Simplifying your schedule allows you to dedicate more time and energy to the activities and people that matter most.
    o **Learn to Say No**: Practice saying no to commitments and activities that don't align with your priorities. This empowers you to protect your time and focus on what truly matters.

3. **Mindful Living**:

    o **Practice Mindfulness**: Engage in mindfulness practices such as meditation, deep breathing, and mindful walking. These practices help you stay present and fully appreciate each moment, reducing stress and increasing satisfaction.
    o **Limit Distractions**: Reduce distractions such as excessive screen time and social media. Create intentional spaces and times for relaxation, creativity, and connection with loved ones.

4. **Nurture Relationships**:

- **Quality Time**: Prioritize spending quality time with family and friends. Meaningful connections and shared experiences enrich your life and provide emotional support.
- **Express Gratitude**: Regularly express gratitude for the people and experiences that bring you joy. This strengthens relationships and fosters a positive outlook.

5. **Engage in Fulfilling Activities**:

   - **Pursue Passions**: Dedicate time to activities that you are passionate about and that bring you joy. Whether it's a hobby, volunteer work, or learning something new, engaging in fulfilling activities enhances your overall happiness.
   - **Balance Leisure and Productivity**: Find a balance between leisure activities and productive pursuits. Both are important for a fulfilling and well-rounded life.

Simplifying your life through decluttering, downsizing, and focusing on what truly matters can lead to greater peace, happiness, and fulfillment in retirement. Embrace the journey of simplifying your life and enjoy the profound benefits it brings to your overall well-being.

Chapter 24

Secret 24: Pursuing Creative Outlets

Engaging in creative activities is a powerful way to enrich your retirement years. Creative outlets such as arts and crafts, music, and writing can bring immense joy, stimulate your mind, and provide a sense of accomplishment. This section explores the benefits of pursuing creative outlets and offers guidance on how to engage in arts and crafts, explore music, and indulge in writing.

Engaging in Arts and Crafts

1. **Benefits of Arts and Crafts**:
    - **Stress Relief**: Engaging in arts and crafts can be a therapeutic activity, reducing stress and promoting relaxation. The repetitive motions and focus required can help calm the mind and provide a sense of peace.
    - **Enhanced Creativity**: Participating in creative projects stimulates your imagination and encourages you to think

outside the box. This can lead to new ideas and innovative solutions in other areas of your life.
- **Improved Motor Skills**: Working with your hands on projects such as painting, knitting, or woodworking can improve fine motor skills and hand-eye coordination.
- **Sense of Achievement**: Completing a craft project gives you a tangible sense of accomplishment and pride in your work.

2. **How to Get Started**:

- **Choose Your Medium**: Identify the types of arts and crafts that interest you. This could include painting, drawing, knitting, crocheting, woodworking, pottery, or jewelry making. Start with one medium and explore others as you gain confidence.
- **Gather Supplies**: Invest in the necessary supplies for your chosen craft. Many hobbies require only basic materials to get started, and you can expand your collection as you progress.
- **Take Classes**: Join a local or online class to learn new techniques and connect with

fellow enthusiasts. Classes provide structure, guidance, and inspiration.
- **Create a Dedicated Space**: Set up a space in your home where you can work on your projects without interruptions. A dedicated creative space helps you stay organized and focused.
- **Enjoy the Process**: Focus on the joy of creating rather than striving for perfection. Embrace the learning process and allow yourself to make mistakes and learn from them.

Exploring Music

1. **Benefits of Music**:

    - **Emotional Expression**: Music allows you to express emotions and connect with others on a deep, emotional level. Whether you're playing an instrument, singing, or listening to music, it can be a powerful outlet for feelings and experiences.
    - **Cognitive Stimulation**: Learning to play an instrument or reading music stimulates your brain, improving memory, concentration, and cognitive abilities.

- **Social Interaction**: Participating in musical groups or attending concerts provides opportunities to meet new people and build social connections.
- **Physical Benefits**: Playing an instrument can improve coordination and fine motor skills. Singing can enhance breathing and lung capacity.

2. **How to Get Started**:

    - **Choose Your Instrument**: Decide which instrument you'd like to learn or continue playing. Consider your interests, physical capabilities, and budget. Common choices include piano, guitar, violin, flute, or voice.
    - **Take Lessons**: Enroll in lessons with a qualified instructor to receive personalized guidance and feedback. Online tutorials and apps can also be valuable resources for learning at your own pace.
    - **Practice Regularly**: Dedicate regular time to practice. Consistent practice is essential for improvement and building muscle memory.
    - **Join a Group**: Look for local music groups, choirs, or bands to join. Playing

with others enhances your skills and provides a sense of community.
- **Explore Different Genres**: Listen to and play a variety of musical genres. Exploring different styles broadens your musical horizons and keeps your practice sessions interesting.

Indulging in Writing

1. **Benefits of Writing**:

    - **Self-Expression**: Writing provides a platform for expressing your thoughts, feelings, and experiences. It can be deeply therapeutic and help you process emotions.
    - **Mental Stimulation**: Writing engages your brain, improving cognitive functions such as memory, critical thinking, and creativity.
    - **Personal Growth**: Reflective writing, such as journaling, encourages self-awareness and personal growth. It helps you gain insight into your thoughts and behaviors.
    - **Legacy Building**: Writing allows you to document your life story, experiences, and

wisdom, creating a legacy for future generations.

2. **How to Get Started**:

    o **Choose Your Format**: Decide on the type of writing that interests you. Options include journaling, poetry, short stories, memoirs, essays, or even blogging. Each format offers unique opportunities for self-expression and creativity.
    o **Set Writing Goals**: Establish clear writing goals to keep yourself motivated and focused. This could be a daily word count, a weekly blog post, or completing a chapter of your memoir.
    o **Create a Writing Routine**: Designate a specific time each day or week for writing. Consistency helps build a writing habit and enhances your skills over time.
    o **Join a Writing Group**: Connect with other writers through local or online writing groups. Sharing your work and receiving feedback can provide inspiration, support, and new perspectives.
    o **Seek Inspiration**: Draw inspiration from your own experiences, nature, books, or

other forms of art. Keep a notebook handy to jot down ideas and observations.

Pursuing creative outlets such as arts and crafts, music, and writing can significantly enhance your retirement experience. These activities provide emotional expression, cognitive stimulation, and a sense of accomplishment. By engaging in creative projects, you can reduce stress, improve mental and physical health, and foster social connections.

Chapter 25

Secret 25: Strengthening Spirituality

Strengthening your spirituality during retirement can deepen your sense of purpose, provide inner peace, and nurture your overall well-being. Exploring spiritual practices and finding inner peace are essential aspects of this journey.

Exploring Spiritual Practices

1. **Benefits of Spirituality**:

    - **Sense of Purpose**: Spiritual practices can provide clarity about life's purpose and meaning, helping you navigate transitions and challenges with greater resilience.
    - **Inner Peace**: Engaging in spiritual activities such as meditation, prayer, or reflection can promote a sense of calmness and tranquility, reducing stress and anxiety.
    - **Connection with Others**: Many spiritual traditions emphasize community and connection. Engaging in spiritual

practices can foster meaningful relationships and a sense of belonging.
- **Personal Growth**: Spirituality encourages self-reflection and personal growth, allowing you to explore your values, beliefs, and identity.

2. **How to Explore Spiritual Practices**:

    - **Reflect on Beliefs**: Take time to reflect on your beliefs and values. Consider what spirituality means to you and how you can incorporate it into your daily life.
    - **Practice Meditation**: Meditation is a powerful tool for cultivating mindfulness and deepening your spiritual connection. Find a quiet space, sit comfortably, and focus on your breath or a mantra.
    - **Engage in Prayer**: If prayer is part of your spiritual tradition, set aside time each day to pray and connect with your beliefs.
    - **Attend Services or Gatherings**: Participate in religious services, spiritual retreats, or community gatherings. These events provide opportunities for learning, reflection, and connection with others who share similar beliefs.

- **Explore Nature**: Spending time in nature can be a spiritual experience. Take walks in natural surroundings, practice mindfulness, and appreciate the beauty and serenity of the environment.

Finding Inner Peace

1. **Practices for Inner Peace**:
   - **Mindfulness**: Practice mindfulness techniques to stay present and focused on the current moment. Mindfulness helps reduce stress and promotes a sense of inner calm.
   - **Yoga**: Engage in gentle yoga practices to improve flexibility, balance, and mental clarity. Yoga combines physical movement with breath awareness, fostering relaxation and peace.
   - **Journaling**: Keep a spiritual journal to record your thoughts, feelings, and insights. Reflect on your experiences, challenges, and moments of gratitude.
   - **Gratitude Practice**: Cultivate a daily gratitude practice to appreciate the blessings in your life. Acknowledge and

express gratitude for relationships, experiences, and simple joys.
- **Volunteer Work**: Engaging in volunteer activities that align with your values can provide a sense of purpose and fulfillment, contributing to inner peace.

2. **Creating a Sacred Space**:

    - **Designate a Quiet Space**: Create a dedicated space in your home where you can practice meditation, prayer, or reflection without distractions.
    - **Decorate Mindfully**: Decorate your sacred space with items that inspire and uplift you, such as candles, incense, sacred symbols, or meaningful artwork.
    - **Set Intentions**: Use your sacred space to set intentions for personal growth, healing, or connection with your spiritual beliefs.

Strengthening your spirituality during retirement can enhance your overall well-being and provide a deeper sense of fulfillment and peace. By exploring spiritual practices such as meditation, prayer, and reflection, and by cultivating inner peace through mindfulness, gratitude, and connection with nature, you can enrich your spiritual journey. Embrace spirituality as a path to personal growth, clarity of purpose, and a profound connection with yourself and others during this meaningful phase of life.

Part 6: Ensuring Long-Term Happiness

Chapter 26

Secret 26: Maintaining a Positive Attitude

A positive attitude is a powerful tool that can significantly enhance your happiness and overall well-being during retirement. The power of positive thinking and the ability to overcome negative thoughts are crucial for ensuring long-term happiness. This section explores the benefits of maintaining a positive attitude and offers strategies for cultivating positivity and managing negativity.

Power of Positive Thinking

1. **Benefits of Positive Thinking**:

    - **Improved Health**: Positive thinking can boost your immune system, lower stress levels, and reduce the risk of chronic illnesses. It promotes overall physical health and longevity.
    - **Enhanced Well-Being**: A positive outlook enhances your mental and emotional well-being, increasing happiness, satisfaction, and resilience.

- **Better Relationships**: Positive individuals tend to attract and maintain healthier relationships. Optimism fosters empathy, kindness, and effective communication.
- **Increased Motivation**: Positive thinking boosts motivation and drive, helping you pursue goals, embrace challenges, and maintain a proactive approach to life.

2. **How to Cultivate Positive Thinking**:

    - **Practice Gratitude**: Regularly acknowledge and appreciate the good things in your life. Keep a gratitude journal and write down three things you are grateful for each day.
    - **Surround Yourself with Positivity**: Spend time with positive, supportive people who uplift and inspire you. Limit exposure to negative influences and environments.
    - **Focus on Solutions**: When faced with challenges, focus on finding solutions rather than dwelling on problems. This proactive approach encourages optimism and resilience.
    - **Celebrate Small Wins**: Acknowledge and celebrate your achievements, no

matter how small. Recognizing progress reinforces a positive mindset.
- **Engage in Positive Self-Talk**: Replace negative self-talk with affirmations and encouraging statements. Remind yourself of your strengths, achievements, and potential.

Overcoming Negative Thoughts

1. **Understanding Negative Thoughts**:

   - **Identify Triggers**: Recognize situations, people, or events that trigger negative thoughts. Understanding your triggers helps you anticipate and manage them effectively.
   - **Acknowledge Emotions**: Allow yourself to feel and acknowledge negative emotions without judgment. Suppressing emotions can lead to greater stress and anxiety.

2. **Strategies to Overcome Negative Thoughts**:

   - **Challenge Negative Thoughts**: Question the validity of negative thoughts. Ask yourself if they are based on facts or

assumptions. Replace irrational thoughts with balanced, realistic perspectives.
- **Practice Mindfulness**: Engage in mindfulness practices to stay present and aware of your thoughts and emotions. Mindfulness helps you observe negative thoughts without getting caught up in them.
- **Use Cognitive Behavioral Techniques**: Apply cognitive-behavioral techniques to reframe negative thoughts. Replace them with positive, constructive alternatives.
- **Limit Negative Influences**: Reduce exposure to negative news, social media, and people who consistently bring negativity into your life.
- **Engage in Relaxation Techniques**: Practice relaxation techniques such as deep breathing, meditation, or yoga to calm your mind and reduce the impact of negative thoughts.

3. **Building Resilience**:
    - **Develop a Support Network**: Build a strong support network of family, friends, and mentors who can provide encouragement and perspective during challenging times.

- **Set Realistic Expectations**: Set realistic expectations for yourself and others. Accept that setbacks and challenges are a part of life, and view them as opportunities for growth.
- **Focus on Strengths**: Concentrate on your strengths and achievements rather than dwelling on weaknesses and failures. Emphasize your capabilities and potential.

Maintaining a positive attitude is essential for ensuring long-term happiness during retirement. The power of positive thinking can improve your health, well-being, relationships, and motivation. By practicing gratitude, surrounding yourself with positivity, and focusing on solutions, you can cultivate a positive mindset. Additionally, overcoming negative thoughts through mindfulness, cognitive-behavioral techniques, and relaxation practices can enhance your resilience and overall happiness.

Chapter 27

Secret 27: Setting New Goals and Challenges

Setting new goals and embracing challenges are essential for a fulfilling and dynamic retirement. Goals provide direction and purpose, while challenges stimulate personal growth and keep life exciting. This section delves into the importance of goal-setting and offers strategies for taking on new challenges during retirement.

Importance of Goal-Setting

1. **Purpose and Direction**:
    - **Sense of Purpose**: Goals give your life purpose and meaning, helping you stay motivated and focused. They provide a reason to get up each morning and pursue your passions.
    - **Clarity and Focus**: Setting clear goals helps you prioritize your activities and concentrate your efforts on what truly matters. It prevents aimlessness and enhances productivity.

2. **Personal Growth**:

    o **Continuous Learning**: Goals encourage you to learn new skills and acquire knowledge. This continuous learning process keeps your mind sharp and engaged.
    o **Self-Improvement**: Achieving goals fosters a sense of accomplishment and boosts self-esteem. It encourages you to strive for excellence and personal growth.

3. **Enhanced Well-Being**:

    o **Mental and Emotional Health**: Working towards meaningful goals promotes mental and emotional well-being. It reduces the risk of depression and anxiety by providing a sense of purpose and achievement.
    o **Physical Health**: Goals related to physical health, such as fitness or wellness targets, motivate you to maintain a healthy lifestyle.

4. **Social Connections**:

    o **Building Relationships**: Goals that involve social activities, such as joining clubs or volunteering, help you build and maintain relationships. These connections contribute to a sense of belonging and community.

Taking on New Challenges

1. **Benefits of Embracing Challenges**:

   - **Stimulated Mind**: Challenges keep your mind active and engaged, promoting cognitive health. They encourage problem-solving, creativity, and critical thinking.
   - **Adaptability and Resilience**: Facing challenges enhances your adaptability and resilience. It prepares you to handle unexpected changes and setbacks with confidence.
   - **Sense of Accomplishment**: Overcoming challenges brings a profound sense of accomplishment and pride. It boosts your self-confidence and reinforces your ability to tackle future obstacles.

2. **How to Embrace New Challenges**:

   - **Identify Areas of Interest**: Explore areas that interest you and where you want to

grow. This could be related to hobbies, skills, travel, or community involvement.
- **Set Specific Goals**: Break down your challenges into specific, manageable goals. Clear and achievable targets make the process less daunting and more attainable.
- **Take Small Steps**: Start with small steps to build confidence and momentum. Gradually increase the difficulty of your challenges as you gain experience and capability.
- **Seek Support**: Don't hesitate to seek support from friends, family, or mentors. Their encouragement and guidance can help you navigate challenges and stay motivated.
- **Stay Positive**: Maintain a positive attitude and view challenges as opportunities for growth. Embrace the learning process and celebrate your progress, no matter how small.

3. **Examples of New Challenges**:
   - **Learn a New Skill**: Take up a new hobby or learn a new language. Enroll in online courses or local classes to expand your knowledge and capabilities.

- **Physical Challenges**: Set fitness goals, such as running a marathon, hiking a challenging trail, or participating in a new sport. Physical challenges improve health and build resilience.
- **Travel Adventures**: Plan trips to new destinations, whether local or international. Traveling exposes you to new cultures, experiences, and perspectives.
- **Volunteer Work**: Take on volunteer roles that challenge you to use your skills and knowledge in new ways. Volunteering provides a sense of purpose and community involvement.
- **Creative Projects**: Engage in creative projects such as writing a book, painting, or starting a blog. These projects allow you to express yourself and share your passions with others.

Setting new goals and embracing challenges are vital for a fulfilling and vibrant retirement. Goals provide purpose, clarity, and direction, while challenges stimulate personal growth and resilience. By identifying areas of interest, setting specific goals, and taking on new challenges, you can enhance your mental, emotional, and physical well-being. Embrace this exciting phase of life with enthusiasm and a positive attitude, and enjoy the sense of accomplishment and fulfillment that comes with pursuing new goals and overcoming challenges.

Chapter 28

Secret 28: Celebrating Milestones and Achievements

Celebrating milestones and achievements is an essential practice for maintaining a positive outlook and enhancing overall happiness during retirement. Acknowledging and celebrating your successes and reflecting on your accomplishments can provide motivation, boost self-esteem, and foster a sense of fulfillment. This section explores the importance of celebrating milestones and offers strategies for effectively acknowledging and reflecting on your achievements.

Acknowledging and Celebrating Successes

1. **Benefits of Celebration**:

    - **Enhanced Motivation**: Celebrating achievements reinforces your efforts and motivates you to pursue new goals. Recognizing progress and success

encourages continued growth and perseverance.
- **Increased Happiness**: Celebrations create joyful and memorable experiences that contribute to your overall happiness. They allow you to savor positive moments and appreciate your journey.
- **Boosted Self-Esteem**: Acknowledging your accomplishments reinforces your self-worth and confidence. It helps you recognize your capabilities and strengths.
- **Strengthened Relationships**: Sharing your successes with friends and family strengthens your relationships and creates a supportive and encouraging environment.

2. **Ways to Celebrate Successes**:

- **Personal Rewards**: Treat yourself to something special as a reward for your hard work. This could be a favorite meal, a relaxing day at the spa, or a new item you've been wanting.
- **Sharing with Loved Ones**: Celebrate your achievements with loved ones. Host a small gathering, share your news over a meal, or simply call a friend to share your excitement.

- **Creating Traditions**: Establish personal or family traditions for celebrating milestones. Whether it's a yearly celebration of achievements or a special ritual for each success, traditions add meaning to your celebrations.
- **Documenting Successes**: Keep a record of your achievements in a journal or scrapbook. Documenting your successes allows you to revisit and reflect on them, providing ongoing inspiration.
- **Public Recognition**: Share your accomplishments publicly if appropriate. This could be through social media, community newsletters, or other platforms where you can inspire and encourage others.

Reflecting on Accomplishments

1. **Importance of Reflection**:

   - **Personal Growth**: Reflecting on your accomplishments allows you to assess your growth and progress. It helps you understand what you've learned and how you've developed over time.

- **Understanding Success**: Reflection helps you analyze the factors that contributed to your success. Understanding what worked well can guide your future efforts and decision-making.
- **Building Gratitude**: Reflecting on your achievements fosters a sense of gratitude for the opportunities, support, and experiences that led to your success. Gratitude enhances overall well-being and happiness.

2. **How to Reflect on Accomplishments**:

   - **Journaling**: Keep a journal dedicated to your achievements. Write about each milestone, the journey to reach it, and the emotions you experienced. Reflect on the challenges you overcame and the lessons you learned.
   - **Mindful Meditation**: Practice mindful meditation to reflect on your accomplishments. Sit in a quiet space, focus on your breath, and gently bring your achievements to mind. Reflect on the feelings of pride, gratitude, and fulfillment they bring.
   - **Discussion with Mentors**: Discuss your accomplishments with mentors or trusted

friends. Their perspectives and feedback can provide valuable insights and help you see your achievements in a new light.
- **Creating a Vision Board**: Visualize your achievements by creating a vision board. Include images, quotes, and mementos that represent your milestones. Display it where you can see it regularly as a reminder of your success.
- **Annual Review**: Conduct an annual review of your accomplishments. Set aside time at the end of each year to review and reflect on the goals you achieved, the progress you made, and the experiences you had.

Chapter 29

Secret 29: Creating a Legacy

Creating a legacy is a powerful way to make a lasting impact on your family, community, and future generations. By sharing your experiences, values, and achievements, you can leave behind a meaningful and inspiring legacy. This section explores the importance of making a lasting impact and offers strategies for documenting your life story.

Making a Lasting Impact

1. **Significance of Legacy**:
    - **Perpetuating Values**: A legacy allows you to pass on your values, beliefs, and life lessons to future generations. It ensures that your principles and wisdom continue to influence and guide others.
    - **Providing Inspiration**: Your story and achievements can inspire others to pursue their dreams, overcome challenges, and lead fulfilling lives. A legacy serves as a source of motivation and encouragement.

- **Creating a Positive Influence**: By contributing to your community, supporting causes you care about, and being a role model, you create a positive impact that extends beyond your lifetime.
- **Connecting Generations**: Sharing your legacy helps bridge generational gaps, fostering a sense of continuity and connection within your family and community.

2. **Ways to Make a Lasting Impact**:

    - **Philanthropy and Charitable Giving**: Support causes and organizations that align with your values. Consider making donations, establishing scholarships, or creating charitable foundations to make a lasting difference.
    - **Mentorship and Teaching**: Share your knowledge and experience by mentoring young people or teaching. Your guidance and support can have a profound impact on their personal and professional development.
    - **Community Involvement**: Actively participate in community projects and initiatives. Your contributions can

improve the lives of others and strengthen the social fabric of your community.
- **Advocacy and Activism**: Advocate for social, environmental, or political causes that matter to you. Your efforts can lead to positive changes and inspire others to take action.

Documenting Your Life Story

1. **Importance of Life Story**:

    - **Preserving Memories**: Documenting your life story preserves your memories, experiences, and achievements for future generations. It ensures that your legacy is remembered and cherished.
    - **Sharing Wisdom**: Your life story is a treasure trove of wisdom and insights. By sharing your experiences, you provide valuable lessons and guidance to others.
    - **Celebrating Accomplishments**: Documenting your life story allows you to celebrate your achievements and reflect on the milestones that shaped your journey.

2. **How to Document Your Life Story**:

    o **Writing a Memoir**: Write a memoir that chronicles your life experiences, significant events, and personal reflections. Include anecdotes, lessons learned, and the values that guided your decisions.
    o **Recording Oral Histories**: Record oral histories by sharing your stories in audio or video format. This method captures the nuances of your voice, expressions, and emotions, making your legacy more personal and engaging.
    o **Creating a Family Tree**: Compile a detailed family tree that includes stories, photographs, and historical documents. This visual representation connects your family's past, present, and future.
    o **Making a Scrapbook**: Create a scrapbook that combines photographs, letters, mementos, and written narratives. This creative and visual approach makes your life story tangible and accessible.
    o **Starting a Blog or Website**: Share your life story online through a blog or personal website. This platform allows you to reach a broader audience and

continuously update your story as you create new memories.

3. **Involving Family and Friends**:

    o **Collaborative Storytelling**: Involve your family and friends in documenting your life story. Encourage them to share their perspectives, memories, and experiences that highlight your impact on their lives.
    o **Intergenerational Projects**: Engage in intergenerational projects where older and younger family members collaborate to document and preserve family history. This fosters a deeper understanding and connection between generations.

Creating a legacy is a meaningful way to make a lasting impact and ensure that your values, achievements, and wisdom are remembered and cherished. By engaging in philanthropy, mentorship, community involvement, and advocacy, you can create a positive influence that extends beyond your lifetime. Documenting your life story through memoirs, oral histories, scrapbooks, and digital platforms preserves your legacy for future generations. Embrace the opportunity to create a legacy that inspires, guides, and connects others, leaving a lasting mark on the world.

Chapter 30

Secret 30: Enjoying the Journey

Embracing the joy of retirement and living in the moment are essential components of a fulfilling and happy life in your golden years. Retirement is a time to savor the fruits of your labor, explore new opportunities, and find contentment in everyday experiences. This section focuses on the importance of enjoying the journey and offers strategies for living in the moment.

Embracing the Joy of Retirement

1. **Appreciating Your Achievements**:

    - **Reflect on Your Accomplishments**: Take time to reflect on your life's work and the goals you've achieved. Celebrate your successes and appreciate the efforts that brought you to this point.
    - **Express Gratitude**: Cultivate a sense of gratitude for the opportunities and experiences that have shaped your life. Recognize the people and events that have contributed to your journey.

2. **Exploring New Opportunities**:

- **Pursue Passions and Hobbies**: Retirement provides the freedom to explore interests and hobbies that you may have set aside during your working years. Whether it's painting, gardening, or learning a new instrument, immerse yourself in activities that bring you joy.
- **Travel and Adventure**: Take advantage of the flexibility retirement offers to travel and explore new places. Discovering new cultures and environments can be incredibly enriching and fulfilling.

3. **Prioritizing Health and Well-Being**:

    - **Stay Physically Active**: Engage in regular physical activities that you enjoy. Exercise not only keeps you healthy but also boosts your mood and energy levels.
    - **Nurture Mental Health**: Practice self-care and engage in activities that promote mental well-being. Meditation, mindfulness, and relaxation techniques can help you maintain a positive outlook.

4. **Building Meaningful Relationships**:

- **Strengthen Bonds**: Spend quality time with family and friends. Strengthening these relationships can bring immense joy and a sense of belonging.
- **Make New Connections**: Join clubs, groups, or volunteer organizations to meet new people and expand your social circle. Building new relationships can lead to rewarding experiences and friendships.

Living in the Moment

1. **Mindfulness and Presence**:

    - **Practice Mindfulness**: Mindfulness involves focusing on the present moment without judgment. Engage in mindfulness practices such as meditation, deep breathing, or simply paying attention to your surroundings.
    - **Savor Everyday Moments**: Take time to appreciate the simple pleasures in life, such as a beautiful sunset, a delicious meal, or a quiet walk in nature. These moments contribute to a sense of contentment and well-being.

2. **Letting Go of Worries**:

- **Release Regrets**: Let go of past regrets and focus on the present. Accept that you cannot change the past, but you can shape your present and future.
- **Manage Anxiety**: Address worries about the future by staying grounded in the present. Plan and prepare for the future, but avoid excessive worrying that detracts from your current enjoyment.

3. **Engaging Fully in Activities**:

    - **Be Present**: Whether you're spending time with loved ones, engaging in a hobby, or simply relaxing, strive to be fully present in the activity. This enhances your enjoyment and deepens your experiences.
    - **Avoid Multitasking**: Focus on one activity at a time to fully immerse yourself in the experience. Multitasking can dilute your attention and reduce the pleasure derived from each activity.

4. **Cultivating a Positive Mindset**:

    - **Focus on Positives**: Shift your focus from what you lack to what you have.

Emphasize the positive aspects of your life and practice gratitude regularly.
- **Embrace Flexibility**: Be open to new experiences and adaptable to change. Flexibility allows you to embrace opportunities and navigate challenges with a positive attitude.

Conclusion

As you stand at the threshold of a new chapter in your life, it's essential to look ahead with optimism and a sense of adventure. Retirement is not just an end but a beginning—a time to explore new horizons, embrace fresh opportunities, and cultivate a life of joy, health, and fulfillment.

Looking Ahead

1. **Embracing the Future**:

    - **Optimism and Excitement**: Approach your retirement with enthusiasm and a positive outlook. The future is filled with possibilities, and your attitude can significantly influence your experience.
    - **Lifelong Learning**: Continue to seek knowledge and growth. Whether through hobbies, travel, or formal education, lifelong learning keeps your mind sharp and your life enriched.
    - **Adapting to Change**: Embrace the changes that come with retirement. Flexibility and adaptability will help you navigate new challenges and seize new opportunities with confidence.

2. **Nurturing Relationships**:

    o **Strengthening Bonds**: Maintain and deepen connections with family and friends. These relationships provide emotional support and enhance your sense of belonging and community.
    o **Building New Connections**: Don't hesitate to meet new people and form new friendships. Social interactions are vital for a fulfilling and happy retirement.

3. **Prioritizing Well-Being**:

    o **Physical Health**: Stay active and prioritize your physical health. Regular exercise, a balanced diet, and adequate sleep are foundational to a vibrant and energetic retirement.
    o **Mental and Emotional Health**: Engage in activities that promote mental wellness, such as meditation, mindfulness, and creative pursuits. Emotional well-being is crucial for overall happiness.

Recap of Key Points

As you reflect on the secrets shared in this book, remember these essential takeaways for a happy, healthy, and wealthy retirement:

1. **Planning Your Retirement**:
    - Start planning early and set realistic goals.
    - Focus on financial planning, budgeting, and managing debt.
    - Maximize Social Security benefits and smartly invest your resources.
    - Create a sustainable withdrawal plan and understand retirement taxes.
    - Engage in thorough estate planning.

2. **Maintaining Physical Health**:
    - Stay physically active and develop a fitness routine.
    - Adopt healthy eating habits and meet your nutritional needs.
    - Focus on mental health, practice mindfulness, and ensure a healthy sleep routine.

3. **Staying Engaged and Happy**:

- Find a purpose and engage in volunteering and community service.
- Build and maintain relationships, travel, and explore new places.
- Embrace lifelong learning, new hobbies, and giving back to the community.

4. **Personal Growth and Fulfillment**:

- Practice gratitude and keep a gratitude journal.
- Embrace change and adaptability, simplify your life, and pursue creative outlets.
- Strengthen your spirituality and maintain a positive attitude.

5. **Ensuring Long-Term Happiness**:

- Set new goals and challenges, celebrate milestones, and create a lasting legacy.
- Enjoy the journey by living in the moment and embracing the joy of retirement.

Encouragement and Final Thoughts

As you embark on this new phase of your life, remember that retirement is an opportunity to rediscover yourself, pursue your passions, and live with purpose and joy. It's a time to cherish your achievements, build new memories, and make a lasting impact. Each day is a gift, and by applying the secrets shared in this book, you can create a retirement that is not only fulfilling but also deeply rewarding.

Take charge of your happiness, prioritize your health, and stay engaged with the world around you. Embrace the journey ahead with an open heart and an adventurous spirit. Your retirement can be the best years of your life—filled with joy, meaning, and endless possibilities.

Here's to a happy, healthy, and wealthy retirement!

www.ingramcontent.com/pod-product-compliance
Lightning Source LLC
Chambersburg PA
CBHW071916210526
45479CB00002B/442